KING LEAR

by William Shakespeare

English Touring Theatre

English Touring Theatre was set up nearly ten years ago with the aim of bringing quality theatre to as many people as possible throughout the country.

In the past nine years we have toured over twenty productions, and gained a reputation for work which is carefully conceived, true to the play and respects its audience. We have won ten major awards, taken eleven productions into London, and worked with some of the most talented and respected artists in the country.

Most of our work has been classical revivals. Our successes include Alan Cumming's *Hamlet*, Kelly Hunter in *As You Like It*, our award winning production of *Hedda Gabler* with Alexandra Gilbreath, both parts of Shakespeare's *Henry IV*, Timothy West and Emma Cunniffe in *The Master Builder*, and Diana Quick and Daniel Evans in *Ghosts*. We also enjoyed considerable success with the world premières of Jonathan Harvey's *Rupert Street Lonely Hearts Club* and *Hushabye Mountain*, which were seen at the Donmar Warehouse and Hampstead Theatre Club. Earlier this year our production of Peter Gill's *The York Realist* enjoyed a sold out run at the Royal Court and transferred to the West End.

At the heart of everything we do is the passionately held belief that quality theatre does not have to be elitist, and that people everywhere expect and deserve the best. This is why in addition to the work on stage we also provide a first class Education Programme to accompany our tours. We are committed to making our work as accessible as possible, and have launched the Friends of English Touring Theatre to celebrate the support we receive from our audience.

We have recently been given a superb new base in London, which we believe will help us do what we are funded for: touring high quality theatre throughout Britain.

Stephen Unwin
Artistic Director

Awards

In its first nine years English Touring Theatre has won ten major awards and received numerous nominations:

BARCLAYS / TMA THEATRE AWARD

BEST ACTOR Alan Cumming *Hamlet*

BEST ACTRESS Kelly Hunter *As You Like It*

BEST TOURING PRODUCTION *Hedda Gabler*

BEST ACTRESS IN A SUPPORTING ROLE Emma Cunniffe *The Master Builder*

SUNDAY TIMES IAN CHARLESON AWARD

FIRST PRIZE Alexandra Gilbreath *Hedda Gabler*

FIRST PRIZE Mark Bazeley *The Seagull*

MANCHESTER EVENING NEWS AWARD

BEST ACTOR Bette Bourne *The Importance of Being Earnest*

BEST NEW PLAY *Rupert Street Lonely Hearts Club*

BEST ACTOR IN A TOURING PRODUCTION Timothy West *The Master Builder*

CITY LIFE AWARD

BEST PLAY *Rupert Street Lonely Hearts Club*

Photography by Ivan Kyncl

Caroline O'Neill, Anne Reid, Ian Mercer and Lloyd Owen in *The York Realist*

visit our web site at www.englishtouringtheatre.co.uk

Cast

Timothy West	KING LEAR
Jessica Turner	GONERIL
Catherine Kanter	REGAN
Rachel Pickup	CORDELIA
Garry Cooper	EARL OF KENT
Patrick Drury	DUKE OF ALBANY
Christopher Campbell	DUKE OF CORNWALL
Michael Cronin	EARL OF GLOUCESTER
Nick Fletcher	EDGAR
Dominic Rickhards	EDMUND
David Cardy	THE FOOL
Andrew Fallaize	KING OF FRANCE
Robert Styles	DUKE OF BURGUNDY
Grant Gillespie	OSWALD
David Glover	GENTLEMAN

All other parts played by Andrew Fallaize, David Glover and Robert Styles.

This production of KING LEAR received its first performance on 23 September 2002 at Malvern Theatres.

Creative & Production Team

Creative Team

DIRECTOR	Stephen Unwin
SET DESIGNER	Neil Warmington
COSTUME DESIGNERS	Mark Bouman and Neil Warmington
LIGHTING DESIGNER	Bruno Poet
ORIGINAL COMPOSITION	Olly Fox
FIGHT DIRECTOR	Terry King
SOUND DESIGNER	Duncan Chave
ASSISTANT DIRECTOR	Tim Stark
ASSOCIATE DESIGNER	Sara Perks
WORKSHOP LEADERS	Kerry Frampton and Paul Warwick
CASTING DIRECTOR	Toby Whale

Production Team

HEAD OF PRODUCTION	Simon Curtis
TECHNICAL MANAGER	Rupert Barth von Wehrenalp
COMPANY STAGE MANAGER	Mike Draper
DEPUTY STAGE MANAGER	Clare Loxley
ASSISTANT STAGE MANAGER	Maxine Foo
TECHNICAL STAGE MANAGER	Andy Stubbs
TOUR TECHNICIAN	Emily Oliver
RELIT ON TOUR BY	Malcolm Rippeth and Jono Kenyon
WARDROBE AND WIG MISTRESS	Susannah Thrush
WARDROBE MISTRESS	Carolyn Daniels
COSTUME ASSISTANT	Louisa Parris
SOUND ASSISTANT	Russell Hepplewhite
BSL INTERPRETERS	Jim Dunne and Caroline Bickerton
AUDIO DESCRIBERS	Vocaleyes: Jane Brambley and Di Langford
PHOTOGRAPHER	Stephen Vaughan
PRINT DESIGN	Dragonfly
SET BUILT AND PAINTED BY	Rupert Blakely, Oxford Theatre Workshop

Costume makers: Paddy Dicky, Anna von Maltzahn, Hilary Wili, Stuart Pearson
Wigs and Hair design: Joanna Taylor, The Wig Service
Make-up supplied by: 'Cosmetics al la carte'

Grateful thanks to: Courtaulds, Royal Exchange Theatre, Manchester and Swarovski

Cast Biographies

Christopher Campbell
DUKE OF CORNWALL

For English Touring Theatre: *As You Like it*, *The Beaux' Stratagem*.

Theatre: *Toast* for Royal Court; *The Night of the Iguana*, *Pygmalion*, *Macbeth*, *The Mountain Giants*, *Dragon*, *Oedipus*, *Mary Stuart*, *Flight* for RNT; *Reader* for Traverse Theatre; *What Every Woman Knows* at West Yorkshire Playhouse; *Translations* for Birmingham Rep; *Communicating Doors* for Library Theatre, Manchester; *A Midsummer Night's Dream* for Globe Theatre, Saskatchewan.

Television: *Coasting*; *Families*; *Sherlock Holmes and the Missing Link*; *Confessional*; *Surprising Stars*.

Film: *Room to Rent*.

Christopher is Senior Reader in the Literary Department of the RNT.

David Cardy
THE FOOL

For English Touring Theatre: *Don Juan*, *The Taming of the Shrew*, *Measure for Measure*.

Theatre: *Bones*, *Nabokov's Gloves*, *On the Edge* at Hampstead Theatre; *What the Butler Saw*, *Why Me?* on national tour; *Troilus and Cressida*, *As You Like it* at Old Vic; *The Tempest*, *Comedy of Errors*, *A Midsummer Night's Dream* at Open Air Theatre, Regent's Park; *The Shallow End* at Royal Court; *Pickwick*, *Double Take*, *Chimes at Midnight*, *Coriolanus* at Chichester Festival Theatre; *Twelfth Night* for Peter Hall Company; *Up For None*, *True Dare Kiss*, *Command or Promise* at RNT; *Chorus of Disapproval* at Lyric, Hammersmith; *Can't Pay Won't Pay* at Criterion; *Progress* at Bush Theatre; *Penny Blue* at Greenwich Theatre; *Taking Steps* at Eastbourne Theatre; *Comedians* at Belgrade Theatre, Coventry.

Television: *Birds of a Feather*; *No Sweat*; *Campaign*; *The Chief*; *Fools Gold*; *New Statesman*; *Stay Lucky*; *Kavanagh QC*; *Silent Witness*; *Absolutely Fabulous*; *Eastenders*; *The Bill*; *Trial by Jury*; *Minder*; *Casualty*; *Safe*.

Film: *Prick Up Your Ears*; *Three Steps to Heaven*; *XTRO*; *Babyjuice Express*.

Garry Cooper
EARL OF KENT

Trained at Drama Centre, London.

Theatre: *Summit Conference*, *Loot*, *Chinchilla* at Citizens Theatre, Glasgow; *Dr Faustus*, *Facades*, *Britannicus* at Lyric, Hammersmith; *Romeo and Juliet*, *Piaf*, *No Orchids for Miss Blandish* at Plymouth Theatre Royal; *Salonika*, *Susan's Breasts* at Royal Court; *Mean Tears*, *Entertaining Strangers* at RNT; *Real Dreams*, *The Danton Affair*, *Wallenstein* for RSC; *The Singing Group* at Chelsea Centre.

Television: *At Home with the Braithwaites*; *The Vice*; *In a Land of Plenty*; *Casualty*; *Harry*; *Darling Buds of May*; *Coronation Street*; *Soldier, Soldier*; *The Bill*; *Bugs*; *Dalziel and Pascoe*; *Emmerdale*; *Peak Practice*; *Heartbeat*; *Lovejoy*.

Film: *Quadrophenia*; *Caravaggio*; *Prick up your Ears*; *An Ungentlemanly Act*; *Walter*; *Jacob*; *Hostile Waters*; *P'Tang Yang Kipperbang*; *Mountains of the Moon*; *Beautiful Thing*.

Radio: *Anthony and Cleopatra*; *Vital Signs*; *Take That Lennon and Sid*; *The Currs*.

Michael Cronin
EARL OF GLOUCESTER

For English Touring Theatre: *Ghosts*, *Love's Labour's Lost*, *The Cherry Orchard*, *The Master Builder*, *Don Juan*, *The Taming of the Shrew*.

Theatre: *An Empty Desk* at Royal Court; *Duet for One*, *Hamlet*, *Due Process of Law* at Dukes, Lancaster; *Hamlet*, *Jail Diary of Albie Sachs*, *Gloo Joo* at Young Vic; *Hedda Gabler* at Octagon, Bolton; *The*

Cast Biographies

Prisoner of Zenda, *The Corn is Green*, *Northanger Abbey* at Greenwich Theatre; *Richard II*, *Henry IV Parts I and II*, *Henry V*, *Henry VI*, *Richard III*, *Coriolanus*, *The Winter's Tale* for ESC; *All My Sons* for OSC; *Hamlet*, *Comedians* at Belgrade Theatre, Coventry; *Timon of Athens* at AJTC Brix Theatre.

Television: *Fawlty Towers*; *Marie Curie*; *Grange Hill*; *Midnight at the Starlight*; *Invasion*; *Tiny Revolution*; *Poirot: The Mysterious Affair at Styles*; *Tom Jones*; *The Mayor of Casterbridge*.

Film: *Jesus of Nazareth*; *Hopscotch*; *Hour of the Pig*; *For My Baby*; *Jeremiah*; *RKO 281*; *The Discovery of Heaven*.

Michael has written two television films *Stealing the Fire* and *No Final Truth*. His first novel *Against the Day* was published by Oxford University Press in July 1998 and was shortlisted for the Angus Book Award. The sequel *Through the Night* will appear in January 2003.

Patrick Drury
DUKE OF ALBANY

Theatre: *Dear Daddy* at The Ambassadors'; *Measure for Measure* at Riverside Studios; *Flying Blind*, *The Key Tag* at Royal Court; *Much Ado About Nothing*, *Don Juan*, *The Prince of Homburg*, *Danton's Death*, *Sergeant Musgrave's Dance*, *Bartholomew Fair*, *Murderers*, *Fuente Ovejuna* at RNT; *The Trinidad Sisters* at Donmar

Warehouse; *Silas Marner* at Orange Tree Theatre; *Coriolanus* for Steven Berkoff Company; *The Memory of Water* at Vaudeville; *Afore Night Come* at Young Vic; *Rebecca* at Vienna English Theatre; *The Seagull* at Theatre Royal, Northampton.

Television: *Father Ted* (three series); *The Men's Room*; *The Politician's Wife*; *Under the Sun*; *Rumpole*; *Moon & Son*; *Inspector Morse*; *Shoot to Kill*; *Breed of Heroes*.

Film: *The Awakening*; *The Nightingale Saga*; *Laughterhouse*.

Andrew Fallaize
KING OF FRANCE

Theatre: *Original Sin* at Crucible Theatre, Sheffield; *The Prince of Homburg* at RSC and Lyric, Hammersmith; *House/Garden* at RNT; *The School For Wives* at BAC and Wimbledon.

Film: *Who Can I Turn To?*

Radio: *The Merry Wives of Windsor*; *How the White King Died*.

Nick Fletcher
EDGAR

Trained at Bristol University

and Webber Douglas.

For English Touring Theatre: *Love's Labour's Lost*, *A Difficult Age*.

Theatre: *Star Quality* at the Apollo; *A Slight Witch*, *Silence* at Birmingham Rep; *All's Well That Ends Well* at Chicago Shakespeare Theater; *A Wife Without a Smile*, *The House Amongst the Stars*, *Court in the Act*, *The Way of the World*, *The Last Thrash*, *Seagulls*, *The Cassilis Engagement* in the 1998/1999 ensemble at Orange Tree Theatre; *Henry V*, *A Chaste Maid in Cheapside* at the Globe; *Burdalane* at BAC; *The Fall* at Chelsea Centre; *Epping Forest* at Theatre Museum.

Television: *Rough Treatment*; *The Visitor*; *Grange Hill*; *After the War*.

Film: *Bring Me the Head of Mavis Davies*.

Radio: *The Women in His Life*; *Passing Men*; *A Magnificent Prospect of The Works*; *Mary Hays in Love*.

For Naxos Audiotapes: *Twelfth Night*, *Henry V*, *Richard II*.

Grant Gillespie
OSWALD

For English Touring Theatre: *Love's Labour's Lost*, *Don Juan*, *The Taming of the Shrew*.

Theatre: *Don Juan* at Crucible Theatre, Sheffield; *The Old Curiosity Shop* at Southwark Playhouse; *Alone*

Cast Biographies

Together at The Mill at Sonning; *The Browning Version* at Arches, Glasgow; *Entertaining Angels* at Tron, Glasgow, Traverse Theatre and BAC; *Easy* at Citizens Theatre, Glasgow; *Chinese Whispers* at Traverse Theatre; *Crush* at Tramway, CCA, Glasgow and ICA; *Dungeon Tales, Cymbeline* on international tour.

Television: *Poirot*; *Midsomer Murders*.

Film: *Horses for Courses*; *Next Stop Paradise*; *Vicinato II*; *Death is not an Option*.

David Glover
GENTLEMAN

Theatre: Seasons at Bristol Old Vic, The Haymarket, Leicester and Scarborough; *The Crucible* at Young Vic; *Faith, Hope and Charity* at Lyric, Hammersmith; *The Day the Bronx Died* at Tricycle Theatre; *Oh Dad Poor Dad* at Piccadilly; *Cause Celebre* at Her Majesty's; *Present Laughter* at Aldwych Theatre; *Devil's Disciple, The Importance of Being Earnest, The Man Who Came to Dinner* at Chichester Festival Theatre; *Bond's Lear, King Lear, Roaring Girl, Anthony and Cleopatra, Tartuffe, Cyrano de Bergerac, Romeo and Juliet, The Winter's Tale, Richard II, The Wizard of Oz, Spring Awakening, Much Ado About Nothing, Merry Wives of Windsor, Cymbeline* for RSC.

Television: *Yes, Prime Minister; Cyrano; Tartuffe; Maigret; Inspector Alleyn; House of Eliott; Lady Audley's Secret; Kavanagh QC; The Lost World; Conspiracy; Redcap.*

Film: *The Ipcress File; Funeral in Berlin; Fahrenheit 451; Follow That Camel; Edward II; Princess Cariboo; Blue Juice; Shooting Fish.*

Radio: *The Trials of Marshall Hall; Plums War.*

Catherine Kanter
REGAN

Theatre: *A Woman of No Importance* on national tour; *A Midsummer Night's Dream, Othello, A Warwickshire Testimony, Pentecost, Peer Gynt, The Wives' Excuse* all for RSC; *All My Sons* at Bristol Old Vic; *Tolstoy* at Aldwych Theatre; *Communicating Doors* at Library Theatre, Manchester; *A Servant of Two Masters* at West Yorkshire Playhouse.

Television: *A+E; Cold Feet; Casualty; Wing and a Prayer; Bugs; The Knock; The New Adventures of Robin Hood; Eastenders.*

Film: *The Heart of Me; A Grey Morning; A Brand for the Burning.*

Radio: *Straw Without Bricks.*

Rachel Pickup
CORDELIA

Trained at National Youth Theatre and RADA

Theatre: *Time and the Conways, The Fall Guy* at Manchester Royal Exchange; *The Sea* at Minerva Theatre, Chichester; *Twelfth Night* at Theatr Clwyd and Cardiff New Theatre; *Barefoot in the Park* at Jermyn Street Theatre; *All's Well that Ends Well* for OSC and on tour; *Three Sisters, Home Truths* at Birmingham Rep; *Fortune's Fool* at Chichester Festival Theatre and on tour; *Way Upstream* at Crucible Theatre, Sheffield; other plays include: *A Midsummer Night's Dream, The Rivals, The Cherry Orchard.*

Television: *The Truth* (currently filming); *Coupling; Victoria and Albert; Relic Hunter; Doctors; No Bananas; Soldier, Soldier.*

Film: *AKA; Basil; ESN.*

Radio: *The Pleutocrat; From Here to Eternity.*

Dominic Rickhards
EDMUND

Theatre: *Romeo and Juliet, Macbeth* for ESC; *Bent, Macbeth, Fuente Ovejuna* at RNT; *The Man of Mode, The Man Who Came to Dinner, Kissing the Pope* for RSC; *The Making of A King* at Farnham Theatre; *Couch Grass, Ribbon* at Watermill Theatre, Newbury; *As You Like It* at Tamara Theatres.

Television: Currently *Night and Day; Holby City; Trust;*

Cast Biographies

Previously *Coronation Street*; *Heartbeat*; *Dangerfield*; *The Bill*; *Doctors*; *Soldier, Soldier*; *Back Up*; *The Specials*; *The Two of Us*.

Film: *Walking on the Moon*.

Radio: *The Cruel Sea*; *Bomber*; *Citizens*; *October Scars the Skin* Season on Radio 4.

Dominic is a RNT Education Associate and has directed numerous productions for ESC's Education Department.

Robert Styles
DUKE OF BURGUNDY

Theatre: *Original Sin* at Crucible Theatre, Sheffield; *A Patriot for Me* at RSC, Barbican; *Chicago* at English Speaking Theatre, Frankfurt; *What the Butler Saw* at Belgrade Theatre, Coventry and York Theatre Royal; *The Importance of Being Earnest*, *Lend Me a Tenor* at York Theatre Royal; *The Wind in the Willows* at Birmingham Rep and Theatr Clwyd; *Crime of the Century*, *A Christmas Carol* at Birmingham Rep; *A Midsummer Night's Dream*, *Twelfth Night*, *The Swaggerer* at Open Air Theatre, Regent's Park; *Breaking the Code*, *Spider's Web*, *Consent* at Haymarket Theatre, Basingstoke.

Television: *Eastenders*; *Bugs*; *Troublemakers*; *Crocodile Snap*.

Film: *To Kill a King*; *Hamlet*.

Radio: *Jim Davis*.

Jessica Turner
GONERIL

Theatre: *Equus*, *Hiawatha*, *Lorenzaccio*, *The Fawn*, *Strider*, *The Ancient Mariner*, *Animal Farm*, *Martine*, *Mrs Warren's Profession*, *Neaptide*, *The Beaux' Stratagem*, *The White Chameleon*, *Speer* at RNT; *The Apple Cart* at Phoenix Theatre; *What You Get and What You Expect* at Lyric, Hammersmith; *Good* at Donmar Warehouse; *Haiti/Rwanda* at Tricycle Theatre; *That Summer* at Hampstead Theatre; *In Order of Appearance*, *Much Ado About Nothing*, *The Last of Mrs Cheney*, *The Silver King* at Chichester Festival Theatre; *My Cousin Rachel* at Farnham Theatre; *Oedipus* at Southampton Theatre; *There's a Small Hotel*, *The Importance of Being Earnest*, *Richard II*, *A Portrait of Sylvia Plath*, *Othello* on tour.

Television: *The Cazalets*; *Midsomer Murders*; *The Ambassador*; *Doomwatch*; *The Cater Street Hangman*; *Doctor Finlay* (two series); *Prime Suspect* (series 1); *Christabel*; *All or Nothing at all*; *The Bill*; *Sam Saturday*; *Conjugal Rights*; *Polterguests*; *A Wing and A Prayer*.

Film: *Hiawatha*; *Mill on the Floss*; *Deeply*.

Timothy West
KING LEAR

For English Touring Theatre: *The Master Builder*, *Henry IV Parts I and II*.

Theatre: *King Lear*, *Luther* at RNT; *The External* at Greenwich Theatre and on tour; *The Birthday Party* at Piccadilly Theatre and on tour; *Twelve Angry Men*, *It's Ralph* at Comedy Theatre; *The Rivals* at Chichester Festival Theatre; *When We Are Married* at Whitehall Theatre; *The Sneeze* at Aldwych Theatre; *A Month in the Country* at Albery Theatre; much work for RSC, Prospect Theatre and Bristol Old Vic.

Television: *Bedtime* (two series); *Station Jim*; *Murder in Mind*; *Midsomer Murders*; *Bramwell*; *Cuts*; *Eleven Men Against Eleven*; *Reith to the Nation*; *Framed*; *Beecham*; *Blore MP*; *When We Are Married*; *Brass*; *What the Butler Saw*; *Churchill and the Generals*; *Horatio Bottomley*; *Edward VII*.

Film: *Beyond Borders*; *The Fourth Angel*; *Iris*; *Villa des Roses*; *102 Dalmatians*; *Joan of Arc*; *Ever After*; *Cry Freedom*; *Agatha*; *Hedda*; *The Day of the Jackal*; *Nicholas and Alexandra*.

Timothy's autobiography *A Moment Towards the End of the Play* is published by Nick Hern Books *I'm Here I Think, Where are you?* (letters) by Coronet.

Timothy was made a CBE in 1984 for services to his profession.

Creative Biographies

Stephen Unwin
DIRECTOR

Founding Artistic Director English Touring Theatre since 1993.

For English Touring Theatre: *Ghosts*, *Love's Labour's Lost*, *The Cherry Orchard*, *The Master Builder*, *Don Juan*, *The Taming of the Shrew*, *A Difficult Age*, *The Seagull* (also Donmar Warehouse), *Henry IV Parts I and II* (also the Old Vic), *Hedda Gabler* TMA Best Touring Production (also Donmar Warehouse), *Macbeth* (also Lyric, Hammersmith and Poland), *The School for Wives* (also Riverside Studios), *As You Like It*, *The Beaux' Stratagem* (also Turkey), *A Doll's House*, *Hamlet* (also Donmar Warehouse), *A Midsummer Night's Dream* (also Lilian Baylis).

Theatre: *The Lottery of Love*, *Torquato Tasso*, *A Yorkshire Tragedy* at Cottesloe for RNT Studio as Resident Director; *The Long Way Round* for RNT; *The Magic Carpet* for RNT Education Department; *Karate Billy Comes Home*, British Premières of *Man to Man*, *The Conquest of the South Pole* for Royal Court; *Elizabeth Gordon Quinn*, *The Orphans' Comedy*, *White Rose*, *Elias Sawney*, *Abel Barebone*, *Shadowing the Conqueror* for Traverse Theatre. London transfers

include: *Sandra/Manon* to Donmar Warehouse; *Kathie and the Hippopotamus*, *White Rose* to Almeida; *Dead Dad Dog* to Royal Court Upstairs. Repertory work includes: *Look Back in Anger*, *Knickers!* at Bristol Old Vic; *Our Country's Good* at Leicester Haymarket; *The Price* for OSC.

Theatre in Europe includes: *Measure for Measure*, *The Comedy of Errors*, Graz; *The Broken Jug*, Antwerp; *Macbeth*, Bochum and Neuss.

Opera: Hans Eisler/Bertold Brecht's *The Decision*, Almeida Music Festival and Radio Three; *The Marriage of Figaro*, *Cosi fan Tutte*, *Lucia Di Lammermoor* for Opera 80; *Scipio* for Guildhall School; *Gianni Schicchi* for ENO; *Il Barbiere di Siviglia* at Royal Opera House; *Albert Herring*, *Falstaff*, *Seraglio*, *Le Nozze di Figaro*, *Don Giovanni* for Garsington Opera.

Writing: *A Pocket Guide to Shakespeare's Plays*, *A Pocket Guide to Twentieth Century Drama*, both for Faber and Faber, and currently writing *A Pocket Guide to Ibsen, Chekhov and Strindberg*, also for Faber and Faber, and *So you want to be a Theatre Director?* for Nick Hern Books.

Neil Warmington
SET AND COSTUME DESIGNER

For English Touring Theatre: *Ghosts*, *Love's Labour's Lost*, *Don Juan*, *The Taming of the Shrew*.

Theatre includes: *The Glass Menagerie*, *Woyzeck*, *Comedians*, *Merlin* at Royal Lyceum, Edinburgh; *Life is a Dream*, *Fiddler on the Roof* at West Yorkshire Playhouse; *Much Ado About Nothing*, *Waiting For Godot* at Everyman, Liverpool; *Much Ado About Nothing* at Queens Theatre; *Life of Stuff* at Donmar Warehouse; *Henry V* for RSC, Stratford and Barbican; *The Tempest* at Contact; *Angels in America* for 7:84 and Traverse Theatre; *Jane Eyre*, *Desire Under the Elms* for Shared Experience and at Tricycle Theatre; *Women Laughing* at Watford Palace; *Passing Places*, *Wiping my Mother's Arse*, *Family*, *King of the Fields*, *Solemn Mass for a Full Moon* at Traverse Theatre; *Crazyhorse*, *Splendour*, *Drowned World*, *Riddance* for Paines Plough; *The Duchess of Malfi* at Theatre Royal, Bath; *Dissent* for 7:84; *Sunset Song* at Theatre Royal, Glasgow (touring).

Opera: *Troilus and Cressida* for Opera North; *Oedipus Rex* for Connecticut State Opera; *Le Nozze di Figaro* for Garsington Opera.

Creative Biographies

Awards include: Three TMA Awards for Best Design; The Linbury Prize for Stage Design; Five Edinburgh Fringe Firsts; Sir Alfred Munnings Florence Prize for Painting; Noel Machine Memorial Prize for Painting.

Mark Bouman
COSTUME DESIGNER

For English Touring Theatre: *Ghosts*, *Fool for Love*, *Love's Labour's Lost*, *The Cherry Orchard*, *Don Juan*, *The Taming of the Shrew*, *A Difficult Age*, *Shellfish*, *Measure for Measure*, *The Seagull*, *Henry IV Parts I and II*.

Theatre: *Lady Windermere's Fan* at Theatre Royal Haymarket; *Cabaret*, *Song of Singapore*, *The Glass Menagerie*, *Divorce Me Darling* at Chichester Festival Theatre; *Twelfth Night*, *Bravely Fought the Queen*, *Border Crossings*, *1000 Broken Mirrors* at Oval House.

Opera includes: *Fidelio*, *La Boheme*, *Zoë* at Glyndebourne; *Don Giovanni*, *Le Nozze di Figaro* at Garsington; *Manon Lescaut*, *Il Trittico*, *Il Giasone* at Spoleto Festival, USA; *Tosca*, *Carmen*, *La Bohème* at Holland Park; *The Marriage of Figaro* at Stowe; *The Tsarina's Shoes* at Guildhall.

Television: *Lenny Henry Show*; *Comic Relief*; *Mike and Angelo*; *Pottermus Park*; also numerous commercials.

Film: *Orlando*.

Bruno Poet
LIGHTING DESIGNER

For English Touring Theatre: *Love's Labour's Lost*, *The Cherry Orchard*, *Don Juan*, *The Taming of the Shrew*.

Theatre includes: *Les Blancs*, *The Homecoming* at Manchester Royal Exchange; *The Birthday Party*, *Sexual Perversity in Chicago*, *The Shawl* at Crucible Theatre, Sheffield; *Island of Slaves* at Lyric, Hammersmith; *So Long Life*, *The External* at Theatre Royal, Bath and on tour; *Neville's Island* at Watford Palace; *Royal Supreme*, *Musik* at Plymouth Theatre Royal; *Antarctica*, *Tess of the D'Urbevilles* at Savoy.

Opera/Dance includes: Five seasons at Garsington Opera; *Fidelio* for De Vlaamse Opera; *Orfeo Et Euridice* for Opera National Du Rhin; *La Traviata* for ETO; *Macbeth* for North Jutland Opera Company; *The Yeoman of the Guard* for British Youth Opera; *The Turn of the Screw* at Brighton Festival; *Hansel and Gretal* at Wilton's Music Hall; dance pieces for Rambert, Walker Dance at Traverse Theatre.

Olly Fox
ORIGINAL COMPOSITION

For English Touring Theatre: *The Caretaker*, *The Taming of the Shrew*.

Recent theatre includes: *Where Do We Live* for Royal Court; *Bones*, *Hand in Hand* (sound design) for Hampstead Theatre.

Other theatre includes: *The Way of the World*, *Eliza's House*, *Two Clouds Over Eden* at Manchester Royal Exchange; *The Duchess of Malfi*, *Macbeth*, *Equus*, *The Winter's Tale* at Salisbury Playhouse; *The Good Woman of Setzuan* at RNT; *The Three Birds* at Gate Theatre; *Cold* for Ashton Contemporary Theatre Group; *See-Saw* for Quarantine at The Tramway, Glasgow; *Lifegame* for Improbable on national tour; *The Wasp Factory*, *But the Living are Wrong in the Sharp Distinctions They Make* for Northern Stage; *Mother Courage*, *A Midsummer Night's Dream*, *The Mill on the Floss* for Contact Theatre.

Olly has also written scores for many other theatre companies.

Creative Biographies

Radio includes: *Shirley, Millport, Through the Looking Glass, The Ghost of Federico Garcia Lorca, Wainewright the Poisoner, The Echoing Waters, Desire Lines* for BBC Radio 3 and 4.

Television includes: *The Royal Collection* for the BBC.

Terry King
FIGHT DIRECTOR

For English Touring Theatre: *Macbeth, As You Like It, Hamlet.*

Theatre: *Troilus and Cressida, Richard III, Romeo and Juliet, Cymbeline, Pericles, Julius Ceasar, Coriolanus, Henry V, Hamlet, A Patriot for Me, The White Devil, Comedy of Errors, Twelfth Night, Othello, Henry IV Parts I and II, Bite of the Night, Singer, A Midsummer Night's Dream, Henry IV Parts I, II and III, As You Like It, Macbeth* for RSC; *Fool for Love, The Murderers, King Lear, The Sea, Othello, The Birthday Party, Carousel, The Cripple of Inishman, The Riot, Chips and Everything, Battle Royal, London Cuckolds, Waiting for Godot, Ting Tang Mine, Three Men on a Horse, Jacobowski and the Colonel, The Homecoming* for RNT; *Our Country's Good, The Recruiting Officer, The Queen and I, King Lear, Sore Throats, Search and Destroy, Ashes and Sand, Olleana, Berlin Berty, Ourselves Alone, Greenland* at Royal Court.

Opera / Musicals: *Porgy and Bess; Otello; Carmen; Martin Guerre; Jesus Christ Superstar; Oliver; Saturday Night Fever; Spend Spend Spend; West Side Story; Lautrec; Chitty Chitty Bang Bang.*

Television: *The Bill; Casualty; Eastenders; Broken Glass; A Kind of Innocence; Fell Tiger; Scolds Bridal; Fatal Invasion; Nerys Glas; Death of a Salesman; The Widowing of Mrs Holroyd; Measure for Measure; The Mayor of Casterbridge; Lucky Jim; Blue Dove; Rock Face.*

Duncan Chave
SOUND DESIGNER

Sound Design work includes: *The Good Woman of Setzuan, Further Than the Furthest Thing, Widowers' Houses* for RNT; *Lam, Sense and Sensibility* at Northcott Theatre, Exeter; *The Promise* at Everyman, Liverpool.

Other Theatre includes:
As Music Programmer: *Remembrance of Things Past, Candide, Oklahoma!, Troilus and Cressida, Battle Royal* for RNT; *Chitty Chitty Bang Bang, The King and I* in the West End; *Beauty and the Beast, West Side Story* on national tour.

As Musician: (keyboards) *Angels in America Parts 1 and 2, Macbeth, The Tempest, Flight, Powerbook* for RNT.

As Composer: *Ooh Ah Showab Khan, Season of the Snowqueen, Soft Times, Lost for Words, My England* for ARC Theatre Ensemble's productions.

Tim Stark
ASSISTANT DIRECTOR

Theatre: Assistant Director recently on *The Associate, A Prayer for Owen Meany* at RNT; *Push Up* at Royal Court.

Directing: *Bombing People, Signing Off* at Jermyn St Theatre; *Dealt With* at Chelsea Centre; *Heads* at Bridewell Theatre; *Serving It Up, Rafts and Dreams, King John* at Poor School; also directed a workshop of *Metro*, a new musical which he also co-wrote.

Acting credits: *The Natural Cause* at NT Studio; *Across Oka, Mary and Lizzy, Restoration* for RSC; *Making Noise Quietly, Macbeth* for RSC and Almeida Theatre; *A Memory of Two Mondays* at Cockpit Theatre; *Les Liaisons Dangereuses* at Derby Playhouse; *Neville South's Washbag* at Finborough Theatre.

Television: *Guardians; Pie in the Sky; Frankenstein; All Good Things; William Tell; Little Eyolf.*

Creative Biographies

Film: *Heaven's Promise, A Shocking Accident.*

Tim is this year's Cohen Bursary at the NT Studio and English Touring Theatre.

Sara Perks
ASSOCIATE DESIGNER

Trained at Bristol Old Vic Theatre School and University of Kent.

For English Touring Theatre: *Ghosts, The York Realist, The Caretaker, Love's Labour's Lost, Beyond a Joke, The Cherry Orchard, Master Builder.*

Theatre includes: *Romeo and Juliet* for Northcott Theatre, Exeter; *Caucasian Chalk Circle* at Mercury Theatre, Colchester; *Aeroplane Bones* at Bristol Old Vic; *Skylight* at Dukes, Lancaster; *Belle* at Gate Theatre; *Frankie & Tommy* at Lyric, Hammersmith; *The Owl and the Pussycat* at Redgrave Theatre, Bristol; *Union Street* at Plymouth Theatre Royal; *Gringos* at BAC and Bristol Old Vic; *The Old Curiosity Shop* at Southwark Playhouse; *The Lost Domain* Drum Theatre, Plymouth; and the original Edinburgh and London club productions of the cult musical *Saucy Jack and the Space Vixens*; Design Assistant for *Carmen* at Glyndebourne; *Rigoletto* at

Covent Garden; *Alcina* for ENO.

Awards: The John Elvery Theatre Design Award and a BBC Vision Design Award for *A Midsummer Night's Dream* at Redgrave Theatre, Bristol.

Kerry Frampton
WORKSHOP LEADER

Kerry graduated from Bretton Hall College with a BA (Hons) in Theatre Arts.

She has worked as a workshop leader, actor and writer. She has been part of English Touring Theatre's education team for over a year and toured to many schools and colleges across the UK, co-leading the Practitioners Unplugged programme in 2001 and earlier this year devising/leading the workshops for the tour of Ibsen's *Ghosts.* She has also worked with Oldham Theatre Workshop, York's Talented and Gifted programme and Electric Storm. With her own company – Splendid Productions – she offers workshops in devising, improvisation and physical theatre.

Kerry's last project was *Carnival Messiah* at the West Yorkshire Playhouse which she has been involved with since 1994 both as a writer and performer. Previous productions include *A Change*

of *Mind* at Sadlers Wells; *A Midsummer Night's Dream* at Cambridge Arts Theatre; *Paradise* at Moray House Theatre.

Paul Warwick
WORKSHOP LEADER

Theatre Direction: Artistic Director of double Fringe First winning Unlimited Theatre from 1996 until 2001 for whom he directed seven highly acclaimed productions.

As a director: *Act Without Words, The Bacchae, King Lear, Macbeth* for The Workshop Theatre; *The Man of Mode* for In Your Space; Co-directed *Epiceone, The Roaring Girl, The Witch of Edmonton* for Mamamouchi's Miscreants.

As an actor: Performed in *The Swing Left, Scream* for Unlimited; *Too, Love Play, Sleeping Around* for Rose Bruford; *Torch Song Trilogy* at Finborough Theatre; acted in a number of television and film roles including *About a Boy, Tipping the Velvet* and Channel 4's *Spaced*; performs political satire as part of *Pub Quiz.*

Paul is also a freelance drama teacher and University lecturer; has had articles and translations published by NTQ and Methuen Drama.

Theatre for everyone

An Open Door

English Touring Theatre believes quality productions of great drama should be open to all. At the heart of everything we do is our commitment to national touring.

• We believe there should be no contradiction between artistic integrity and public accessibility, and we aim to produce work which is clear and true to the play.

• Although we have no direct control over ticket prices we try to encourage the venues to address this issue as creatively as possible.

• Our education initiatives have earned a national reputation for creative and innovative work involving thousands of young people each year.

• We run a nationwide programme of special events and training courses hosted by established arts professionals.

• We regularly organise pre show talks, post show discussions and workshops which allow members of our audience to gain a deeper insight into the artistic process.

• We provide masterclasses and practical sessions for adults, examining all aspects of language, dramaturgy, historical context and professional theatre practice.

• We offer arts based management training programmes to assist businesses with communication, presentation and interpersonal skills.

Access For All

English Touring Theatre regularly offers events and performances specially designed for visually and hearing impaired audience members. In collaboration with organisations such as Stagesign, SPIT, Minds Eye and Vocaleyes we provide:

• BSL Interpreted and Audio Described performances and events led by qualified professionals.

• Touch Tours providing an audio described introduction to characters, set, costumes and props, followed by a guided tour of the stage where participants are able to touch and feel the materials used to create the world of the play.

The Friends of English Touring Theatre scheme allows our audience to get more involved with the Company.

The support of our Friends is essential to ETT's continued success. We actively encourage our audience to get involved, and we want to give our Friends as many additional benefits as possible. In return we hope our Friends will continue to support us in our aim of touring high quality theatre throughout the country. Every penny you can give will go on stage. Please support us as generously as you can.

Relaunching the Friends scheme earlier this year has proved highly successful, and we are delighted to number Trevor Nunn, Prunella Scales, Emma Thompson, Timothy West and Penelope Wilton amongst our Good and Best Friends. However, as we are now producing four shows a year your support and involvement will be more crucial than ever before.

As a Friend of ETT you will receive regular information about our productions and events and a newsletter containing exclusive articles and information.

£50 Good Friend

For £50 per year, you will receive the benefits enjoyed by Friends, plus:

- Discounts on a wide range of merchandise including books and educational resource materials
- Loyalty discounts - the more years you are a Good Friend the larger the loyalty discounts you will receive
- Exclusive 'Friend Only' ticket discounts at your local theatre for all ETT productions
- Automatic entry into regular prize draws and competitions

£100 Best Friend

For £100 per year, you will receive the benefits enjoyed by Friends and Good Friends, plus:

- Invitations to 'meet the cast and creative team' evenings at a tour venue near to you
- Free programmes and posters mailed direct to your door in advance of the performance
- Your name listed in our programmes
- Invitations to ETT's Christmas Party and other exclusive events

English Touring Theatre

Malvern Theatres

Malvern Theatres, Grange Road,
Malvern, Worcestershire WR14 3HB
Tel 01684 569256
website www.malvern-theatres.co.uk

Malvern Theatres

Nestling at the foot of the Malvern Hills, Malvern Theatres is a major centre for the arts in the West Midlands and the home of the famous Malvern Festivals, founded by Bernard Shaw and Barry Jackson in 1929. In 1998 and 1999, Malvern Theatres was host to two drama festivals brought by the acclaimed Almeida Theatre Company. These festivals included such productions as *Phaedre* with Diana Rigg and Toby Stephens, as well as the world première of Edward Albee's *The Play About The Baby* with Alan Howard and Frances de la Tour. Then in summer 2000, the Royal National Theatre premièred their new production of *Hamlet*, with Simon Russell Beale in the title role and this was followed by the world première of Hugh Whitemore's play *God Only Knows*, starring Derek Jacobi. The 2002 Festival has already seen productions of W Somerset Maugham's *The Circle* with Wendy Craig and Tony Britton and Terence Rattigan's *The Winslow Boy* with Edward Fox and Simon Ward. It now culminates with this new production of *King Lear* with Timothy West.

Malvern Theatres began its close association with English Touring Theatre in 1998 with *The Taming of the Shrew*, which featured Kacey Ainsworth, now known to millions as 'Little Mo' from the BBC drama *EastEnders*. Many fine productions have followed including Ibsen's *The Master Builder* with Timothy West, Chekhov's *The Cherry Orchard* with Prunella Scales, Sam Shepard's *Fool for Love*, Harold Pinter's *The Caretaker* and Ibsen's *Ghosts* with Diana Quick. Malvern Theatres is delighted to be co-producing this major new production with English Touring Theatre.

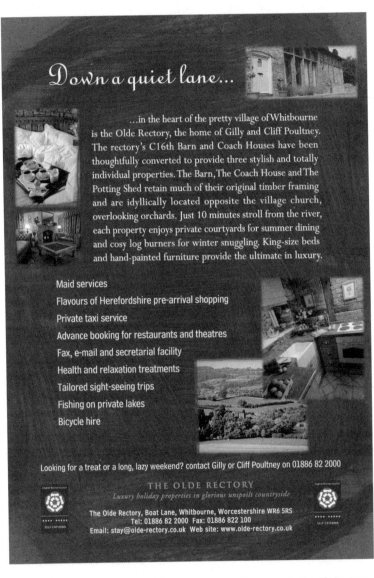
Wishing all at ETT and Malvern Theatres every success with your production of King Lear. We look forward to offering some peace and relaxation to the cast and crew during their stay here.

Gilly and Cliff Poultney - The Olde Rectory
THE ULTIMATE RELAXING BREAK

First published in this edition in 2002 by Oberon Books Ltd.
(incorporating Absolute Classics)
521 Caledonian Road, London N7 9RH
Tel: 020 7607 3637 / Fax: 020 7607 3629
e-mail: oberon.books@btinternet.com

A catalogue record for this book is available from the British Library.

ISBN: 1 84002 322 8

Cover photograph: Stephen Vaughan

Cover design: Dragonfly

Printed in Great Britain by Antony Rowe Ltd, Chippenham.

Contents

Introduction

This text has been prepared for English Touring Theatre's 2002 production of *King Lear*. The aim has been to produce an edition which is clear, straightforward and immediate. I hope it will encourage actors and readers to approach this most familiar of plays with freshness and an open mind.

There is probably more scholarly debate on the text of *King Lear* than any other Shakespeare play. There are several excellent academic editons, which draw on the great tradition of Shakespearean textual studies. But such editions, packed with appendices, learned introductions and editorial quibbles, can be both intimidating and counterproductive. (The Oxford Complete Shakespeare publishes two different versions of the play: *The History of King Lear* and *The Tragedy of King Lear*.) Our text borrows freely from all of these sources. Shakespeare scholars may hate it, but it is an effective working script, assembled for a particular production with particular people at a particular time.

The play has been fairly extensively cut. My chief criterion has been to lose anything which is incomprehensible (my favourite example is Edgar's 'Dauphin, my boy! Boy, cessez; let him trot by.'). I have been severe on the more rhetorical flourishes and those moments when characters recap what we already know. It seems that Shakespeare's audiences were better at listening than we are, but perhaps also needed things spelt out more. I am convinced that a modern production is more likely to engage an audience when the production focusses on what is strictly necessary.

More controversially, I have taken out most of the punctuation marks and limited myself to full stops, commas, question marks and dashes. The fact is that we have very little sense of how Shakespeare himself would have punctuated and the punctuation provided by modern editors follows the conventions of Victorian and modern English. This is alien to Shakespeare. More importantly, it encourages actors to break up the flow of the language and ignores the innate punctuation which is so strongly indicated by the verse.

Most controversially of all, I have removed all the stage directions. A Shakespearean text littered with 'exeunts' and 'tuckets', or 'enter the King with train' and so on, can too easily feel like a kind of Elizabethan theme park. We should discover Shakespeare's dramatic demands from his words, and not from what modern editors think. Shakespeare was an actor himself and his plays were written to be heard and on the stage. It is time for the people who stage these plays today to reclaim his extraordinary texts as their own.

Stephen Unwin
London, September 2002

Characters

KENT

GLOUCESTER

EDMUND

LEAR

GONERIL

REGAN

CORDELIA

ALBANY

CORNWALL

BURGUNDY

FRANCE

EDGAR

OSWALD

FOOL

CURAN

GENTLEMEN

SERVANTS

MESSENGERS

HERALD

CAPTAIN

1

Kent
I thought the King had more affected the Duke of Albany than Cornwall.

Gloucester
It did always seem so to us. But now, in the division of the kingdom, it appears not which of the Dukes he values most, for equalities are so weighed, that curiosity in neither can make choice of either's moiety.

Kent
Is not this your son, my lord?

Gloucester
His breeding, sir, hath been at my charge. I have so often blushed to acknowledge him, that now I am brazed to it.

Kent
I cannot conceive you.

Gloucester
Sir, this young fellow's mother could. Whereupon she grew round-wombed, and had, indeed, sir, a son for her cradle ere she had a husband for her bed. Do you smell a fault?

Kent
I cannot wish the fault undone, the issue of it being so proper.

Gloucester
But I have, sir, a son by order of law, some year elder than this, who yet is no dearer in my account. Though this knave came something saucily into the world before he was sent for, yet was his mother fair, there was good sport at his making, and the whoreson must be acknowledged. Do you know this noble gentleman, Edmund?

Edmund
No, my lord.

Gloucester
My lord of Kent. Remember him hereafter as my
honourable friend.

Edmund
My services to your lordship.

Kent
I must love you and sue to know you better.

Edmund
Sir, I shall study deserving.

Gloucester
He hath been out nine years and away he shall again. The
King is coming.

Lear
Attend my lords of France and Burgundy, Gloucester.

Gloucester
I shall, my liege.

Lear
Meantime we will express our darker purpose.
Give me the map there. Know that we have divided
In three our kingdom and tis our fast intent
To shake all cares and business from our age
Conferring them on younger strengths while we
Unburdened crawl toward death. Our son of Cornwall
And you our no less loving son of Albany
We have this hour a constant will to publish
Our daughters several dowers that future strife
May be prevented now. Tell me my daughters
Since now we will divest us both of rule
Interest of territory, cares of state
Which of you shall we say doth love us most?
That we our largest bounty may extend
Where nature doth with merit challenge.
Goneril, our eldest-born, speak first.

Goneril
Sir, I love you more than words can wield the matter
Dearer than eyesight, space or liberty

Beyond what can be valued rich or rare
No less than life with grace, health, beauty, honour
As much as child e'er loved or father found
A love that makes breath poor and speech unable
Beyond all manner of so much I love you.

Cordelia
What shall Cordelia do? Love and be silent?

Lear
Of all these bounds, even from this line to this
With shadowy forests and with champains riched
With plenteous rivers and wide-skirted meads
We make thee lady. To thine and Albany's issue
Be this perpetual. What says our second daughter
Our dearest Regan, wife to Cornwall? Speak.

Regan
I am made of the self-same metal as my sister
And prize me at her worth. In my true heart
I find she names my very deed of love
Only she comes too short, that I profess
Myself an enemy to all other joys
Which the most precious square of sense possesses
And find I am alone felicitate
In your dear highness love.

Cordelia
                                    Then poor Cordelia.
And yet not so, since I am sure my love's
More richer than my tongue.

Lear
To thee and thine hereditary ever
Remain this ample third of our fair kingdom.
No less in space, validity and pleasure
Than that conferred on Goneril. But now our joy
Although the last not least, to whose young love
The vines of France and milk of Burgundy
Strive to be interest. What can you say to draw
A third more opulent than your sisters? Speak.

Cordelia
Nothing, my lord.

Lear
Nothing?

Cordelia
Nothing.

Lear
Nothing will come of nothing. Speak again.

Cordelia
Unhappy that I am, I cannot heave
My heart into my mouth. I love your majesty
According to my bond, nor more nor less.

Lear
How, how, Cordelia. Mend your speech a little
Lest it may mar your fortunes.

Cordelia
                              Good my lord
You have begot me, bred me, loved me. I
Return those duties back as are right fit
Obey you, love you, and most honour you.
Why have my sisters husbands if they say
They love you all? Haply when I shall wed
That lord whose hand must take my plight shall carry
Half my love with him, half my care and duty.
Sure I shall never marry like my sisters
To love my father all.

Lear
                        But goes thy heart with this?

Cordelia
Ay good my lord.

Lear
                    So young and so untender?

Cordelia
So young my lord and true.

Lear
Let it be so. Thy truth then be thy dower.
For by the sacred radiance of the sun
The mysteries of Hecate and the night
By all the operation of the orbs
From whom we do exist and cease to be
Here I disclaim all my paternal care
Propinquity and property of blood
And as a stranger to my heart and me
Hold thee from this for ever. The barbarous Scythian
Or he that makes his generation messes
To gorge his appetite, shall to my bosom
Be as well neighboured, pitied and relieved
As thou my sometime daughter.

Kent
                                Good my liege –

Lear
Peace Kent.
Come not between the dragon and his wrath.
I loved her most and thought to set my rest
On her kind nursery. Hence and avoid my sight.
Call France. Who stirs?
Call Burgundy. Cornwall and Albany
With my two daughters dowers digest this third.
Let pride which she calls plainness marry her.
I do invest you jointly in my power
Pre-eminence and all the large effects
That troop with majesty. Ourself by monthly course
With reservation of an hundred knights
By you to be sustained, shall our abode
Make with you by due turns. Only we still retain
The name and all the additions to a king.
The sway, revenue, execution of the rest
Beloved sons, be yours. Which to confirm
This coronet part betwixt you.

Kent
                                Royal Lear
Whom I have ever honoured as my king

Loved as my father, as my master followed
As my great patron thought on in my prayers –

Lear
The bow is bent and drawn, make from the shaft.

Kent
Let it fall rather, though the fork invade
The region of my heart. Be Kent unmannerly
When Lear is mad. What wilt thou do, old man?
Thinkst thou that duty shall have dread to speak
When power to flattery bows. To plainness honour's bound
When majesty stoops to folly. Answer my life my judgment
Thy youngest daughter does not love thee least
Nor are those empty-hearted whose low sound
Reverbs no hollowness.

Lear
                              Kent on thy life no more.

Kent
My life I never held but as a pawn
To wage against thy enemies, nor fear to lose it
Thy safety being the motive.

Lear
                              Out of my sight.

Kent
See better Lear and let me still remain
The true blank of thine eye.

Lear
                              Now by Apollo.

Kent
Now by Apollo, King, thou swearst thy gods in vain.

Lear
O vassal, miscreant.

Albany/Cornwall
Dear sir, forbear.

Kent
Kill thy physician and the fee bestow
Upon thy foul disease. Revoke thy doom
Or whilst I can vent clamour from my throat
I'll tell thee thou dost evil.

Lear
                              Hear me, recreant
On thine allegiance hear me.
Since thou hast sought to make us break our vow
Which we durst never yet, and with strained pride
To come between our sentence and our power
Which nor our nature nor our place can bear
Our potency made good, take thy reward.
Five days we do allot thee for provision
To shield thee from diseases of the world
And on the sixth to turn thy hated back
Upon our kingdom. If on the tenth day following
Thy banished trunk be found in our dominions
The moment is thy death. Away by Jupiter
This shall not be revoked.

Kent
Fare thee well King. Since thus thou wilt appear
Freedom lives hence and banishment is here.
The gods to their protection take thee maid
That rightly thinkst and hast most justly said.
And your large speeches may your deeds approve
That good effects may spring from words of love.
Thus Kent, O princes, bids you all adieu
He'll shape his old course in a country new.

Gloucester
Here's France and Burgundy, my noble lord.

Lear
My lord of Burgundy
We first address towards you, who with this king
Hath rivalled for our daughter. What in the least
Will you require in present dower with her
Or cease your quest of love?

Burgundy
>Royal majesty
I crave no more than what your highness offered
Nor will you tender less.

Lear
>Right noble Burgundy
When she was dear to us we did hold her so
But now her price is fallen. Sir, there she stands
If aught within that little seeming substance
Or all of it, with our displeasure pieced
And nothing more, may fitly like your grace
She's there and she is yours.

Burgundy
>I know no answer.

Lear
Will you with those infirmities she owes
Unfriended, new-adopted to our hate
Dowered with our curse and strangered with our oath
Take her or leave her?

Burgundy
>Pardon me royal sir.
Election makes not up on such conditions.

Lear
Then leave her, sir. For by the power that made me
I tell you all her wealth. For you great King
I would not from your love make such a stray
To match you where I hate. Therefore beseech you
To avert your liking a more worthier way
Than on a wretch whom nature is ashamed
Almost to acknowledge hers.

France
This is most strange that she, that even but now
Was your best object, the argument of your praise
Balm of your age, most best, most dearest
Should in this trice of time commit a thing so monstrous
To dismantle so many folds of favour.

Sure her offence must be of such unnatural degree
That monsters it, or your fore-vouched affection
Fallen into taint, which to believe of her
Must be a faith that reason without miracle
Could never plant in me.

Cordelia
I yet beseech your majesty that you make known
It is no vicious blot, murder or foulness
No unchaste action or dishonoured step
That hath deprived me of your grace and favour.
But even for want of that for which I am richer
A still-soliciting eye and such a tongue
As I am glad I have not, though not to have it
Hath lost me in your liking.

Lear
                              Better thou
Hadst not been born than not to have pleased me better.

France
Is it but this, a tardiness in nature
Which often leaves the history unspoke
That it intends to do? My lord of Burgundy
What say you to the lady? Will you have her?
She is herself a dowry.

Burgundy
                              Royal Lear
Give but that portion which yourself proposed
And here I take Cordelia by the hand
Duchess of Burgundy.

Lear
                              Nothing. I have sworn.

Burgundy
I am sorry then you have so lost a father
That you must lose a husband.

Cordelia
Peace be with Burgundy. Since that respects
Of fortune are his love, I shall not be his wife.

France

Fairest Cordelia, that art most rich, being poor
Most choice, forsaken, and most loved, despised
Thee and thy virtues here I seize upon.
Thy dowerless daughter, King, thrown to my chance
Is queen of us, of ours and our fair France.
Not all the dukes in waterish Burgundy
Can buy this unprized precious maid of me.
Bid them farewell, Cordelia, though unkind.
Thou losest here a better where to find.

Lear

Thou hast her, France. Let her be thine, for we
Have no such daughter, nor shall ever see
That face of hers again. Therefore be gone
Without our grace, our love, our benison.
Come, noble Burgundy.

France

Bid farewell to your sisters.

Cordelia

The jewels of our father, with washed eyes
Cordelia leaves you. I know you what you are
And like a sister am most loath to call
Your faults as they are named. Use well our father.
To your professed bosoms I commit him.
But yet alas stood I within his grace
I would prefer him to a better place.
So farewell to you both.

Regan

Prescribe not us our duties.

Goneril

Let your study
Be to content your lord, who hath received you
At fortune's alms. You have obedience scanted
And well are worth the want that you have wanted.

Cordelia
Time shall unfold what plaited cunning hides.
Who cover faults, at last shame them derides.
Well may you prosper.

France
                    Come, my fair Cordelia.

Goneril
Sister, it is not a little I have to say of what most nearly
appertains to us both. I think our father will hence
tonight.

Regan
That's most certain and with you. Next month with us.

Goneril
You see how full of changes his age is. He always loved
our sister most and with what poor judgment he hath
now cast her off appears too grossly.

Regan
Tis the infirmity of his age. Yet he hath ever but slenderly
known himself.

Goneril
The best and soundest of his time hath been but rash.
Then must we look to receive the unruly waywardness
that infirm and choleric years bring with them.

Regan
Such unconstant starts are we like to have from him as
this of Kent's banishment.

Goneril
Pray you, let's hit together. If our father carry authority
with such dispositions as he bears, this last surrender of
his will but offend us.

Regan
We shall further think on it.

Goneril
We must do something, and in the heat.

2

Edmund
Thou nature art my goddess. To thy law
My services are bound. Wherefore should I
Stand in the plague of custom and permit
The curiosity of nations to deprive me
For that I am some twelve or fourteen moon-shines
Lag of a brother? why bastard? wherefore base?
When my dimensions are as well compact
My mind as generous and my shape as true
As honest madam's issue? Why brand they us
With base? with baseness? bastardy? base, base?
Who in the lusty stealth of nature take
More composition and fierce quality
Than doth within a dull, stale, tired bed
Go to the creating a whole tribe of fops
Got tween asleep and wake? Well, then
Legitimate Edgar, I must have your land.
Our father's love is to the bastard Edmund
As to the legitimate. Fine word legitimate.
Well my legitimate, if this letter speed
And my invention thrive, Edmund the base
Shall top the legitimate. I grow, I prosper.
Now, gods, stand up for bastards.

Gloucester
Kent banished thus and France in choler parted?
And the King gone tonight, prescribed his power
Confined to exhibition? All this done
Upon the gad? Edmund, how now, what news?

Edmund
So please your lordship, none.

Gloucester
Why so earnestly seek you to put up that letter?

Edmund
I know no news, my lord.

Gloucester
What paper were you reading?

Edmund
Nothing, my lord.

Gloucester
No? What needed, then, that terrible dispatch of it into your pocket? If it be nothing, I shall not need spectacles.

Edmund
I beseech you, sir, pardon me. It is a letter from my brother, that I have not all overread. And for so much as I have perused, I find it not fit for your overlooking.

Gloucester
Give me the letter, sir.

Edmund
I shall offend, either to detain or give it. The contents, as in part I understand them, are to blame.

Gloucester
Let's see, let's see.

Edmund
I hope, for my brother's justification, he wrote this but as an essay or taste of my virtue.

Gloucester
'This policy and reverence of age makes the world bitter to the best of our times, keeps our fortunes from us till our oldness cannot relish them. I begin to find an idle and fond bondage in the oppression of aged tyranny, who sways, not as it hath power, but as it is suffered. Come to me, that of this I may speak more. If our father would sleep till I waked him, you should enjoy half his revenue for ever, and live the beloved of your brother Edgar.' Conspiracy. 'Sleep till I waked him, you should enjoy half his revenue.' My son Edgar? Had he a hand to write this? a heart and brain to breed it in? When came this to you? who brought it?

Edmund
It was not brought me, my lord. There's the cunning of it.
I found it thrown in at the casement of my closet.

Gloucester
You know the character to be your brother's?

Edmund
If the matter were good, my lord, I durst swear it were
his. But, in respect of that, I would fain think it were not.

Gloucester
It is his.

Edmund
It is his hand, my lord, but I hope his heart is not in the
contents.

Gloucester
Hath he never before sounded you in this business?

Edmund
Never, my lord. But I have heard him oft maintain it to be
fit, that, sons at perfect age, and fathers declining, the
father should be as ward to the son, and the son manage
his revenue.

Gloucester
O villain. His very opinion in the letter. Abhorred villain.
Unnatural, detested, brutish villain. Worse than brutish.
Go, sirrah, seek him. I'll apprehend him. Abominable
villain. Where is he?

Edmund
I do not well know, my lord. I dare pawn down my life for
him, that he hath wrote this to feel my affection to your
honour, and to no further pretence of danger.

Gloucester
Think you so?

Edmund
If your honour judge it meet, I will place you where you
shall hear us confer of this, and by an auricular

assurance have your satisfaction, and that without any further delay than this very evening.

Gloucester
He cannot be such a monster.

Edmund
Nor is not, sure.

Gloucester
To his father, that so tenderly and entirely loves him. Edmund, seek him out, wind me into him, I pray you.

Edmund
I will seek him, sir, presently. Convey the business as I shall find means and acquaint you withal.

Gloucester
These late eclipses in the sun and moon portend no good to us. Love cools, friendship falls off, brothers divide. In cities mutinies, in countries discord, in palaces treason, and the bond cracked twixt son and father. We have seen the best of our time. Find out this villain, Edmund. It shall lose thee nothing. Do it carefully. And the noble and true-hearted Kent banished? His offence? Honesty. Tis strange.

Edmund
This is the excellent foppery of the world, that when we are sick in fortune, we make guilty of our disasters the sun, the moon, and the stars. As if we were villains by necessity, fools by heavenly compulsion, knaves, thieves and treachers by spherical predominance, drunkards, liars, and adulterers by an enforced obedience of planetary influence, and all that we are evil in, by a divine thrusting on. An admirable evasion of whoremaster man, to lay his goatish disposition to the charge of a star. My father compounded with my mother under the dragon's tail, and my nativity was under Ursa Major, so that it follows I am rough and lecherous. Tut, I should have been that I am, had the maidenliest star in the firmament twinkled on my bastardizing. And pat he comes like the

catastrophe of the old comedy. My cue is villanous melancholy, with a sigh like Tom of Bedlam.

Edgar
How now, brother Edmund. What serious contemplation are you in?

Edmund
I am thinking, brother, of a prediction I read this other day, what should follow these eclipses.

Edgar
Do you busy yourself about that?

Edmund
I promise you, the effects he writes of succeed unhappily.

Edgar
How long have you been a sectary astronomical?

Edmund
Come, come, when saw you my father last?

Edgar
Why, the night gone by.

Edmund
Spake you with him?

Edgar
Ay, two hours together.

Edmund
Parted you in good terms? Found you no displeasure in him by word or countenance?

Edgar
None at all.

Edmund
Bethink yourself wherein you may have offended him and at my entreaty forbear his presence till some little time hath qualified the heat of his displeasure.

Edgar
Some villain hath done me wrong.

Edmund
That's my fear. Retire with me to my lodging, from whence
I will fitly bring you to hear my lord speak. Pray you go.
There's my key. If you do stir abroad, go armed.

Edgar
Armed, brother?

Edmund
Brother, I am no honest man if there be any good
meaning towards you. I have told you what I have seen
and heard. Pray you, away.

Edgar
Shall I hear from you anon?

Edmund
I do serve you in this business.
A credulous father and a brother noble
Whose nature is so far from doing harms
That he suspects none. On whose foolish honesty
My practises ride easy. I see the business.
Let me if not by birth have lands by wit
All with me's meet that I can fashion fit.

3

Goneril
Did my father strike my gentleman for chiding of his fool?

Oswald
Yes, madam.

Goneril
By day and night he wrongs me. Every hour
He flashes into one gross crime or other
That sets us all at odds. I'll not endure it.
His knights grow riotous and himself upbraids us
On every trifle. When he returns from hunting

I will not speak with him. Say I am sick.
If you come slack of former services
You shall do well. The fault of it I'll answer.

Oswald
He's coming, madam, I hear him.

Goneril
Put on what weary negligence you please
You and your fellows. I'll have it come to question.
If he dislike it, let him to our sister
Whose mind and mine, I know, in that are one
Not to be over-ruled. Idle old man
That still would manage those authorities
That he hath given away.
Remember what I tell you.

Oswald
                          Well, madam.

Goneril
And let his knights have colder looks among you.
What grows of it, no matter. I'll write straight to my
sister
To hold my very course. Prepare for dinner.

4

Kent
If but as well I other accents borrow
That can my speech defuse, my good intent
May carry through itself to that full issue
For which I razed my likeness. Now banished Kent
If thou canst serve where thou dost stand condemned
So may it come, thy master, whom thou lovest
Shall find thee full of labours.

Lear
Let me not stay a jot for dinner. Go, get it ready. How
now, what art thou?

Kent
A man, sir.

Lear
What dost thou profess?

Kent
I do profess to be no less than I seem, to serve him truly that will put me in trust, to love him that is honest, to converse with him that is wise and says little, to fear judgment, to fight when I cannot choose, and to eat no fish.

Lear
What art thou?

Kent
A very honest-hearted fellow and as poor as the King.

Lear
If thou be as poor for a subject as he is for a king, thou art poor enough. What wouldst thou?

Kent
Service.

Lear
Who wouldst thou serve?

Kent
You.

Lear
Dost thou know me, fellow?

Kent
No, sir. But you have that in your countenance which I would fain call master.

Lear
What's that?

Kent
Authority.

Lear
What services canst thou do?

Kent
That which ordinary men are fit for, I am qualified in, and
the best of me is diligence.

Lear
How old art thou?

Kent
Not so young, sir, to love a woman for singing, nor so old
to dote on her for any thing. I have years on my back
forty eight.

Lear
Follow me. Thou shalt serve me. If I like thee no worse
after dinner, I will not part from thee yet. Dinner, ho,
dinner. Where's my fool? Go you and call my fool hither.
You, you, sirrah, where's my daughter?

Oswald
So please you.

Lear
What says the fellow there? Call the clotpoll back.
Where's my fool, ho? I think the world's asleep.
How now, where's that mongrel?

Gentleman
He says, my lord, your daughter is not well.

Lear
Why came not the slave back to me when I called him?

Gentleman
Sir, he answered me in the roundest manner, he would
not.

Lear
He would not.

Gentleman
My lord, I know not what the matter is. But to my
judgment, your highness is not entertained with that
ceremonious affection as you were wont.

Lear
Ha, sayest thou so?

Gentleman
I beseech you, pardon me, my lord, if I be mistaken. For my duty cannot be silent when I think your highness wronged.

Lear
Thou but rememberest me of mine own conception. I have perceived a most faint neglect of late. I will look further into it. But where's my fool? I have not seen him this two days.

Gentleman
Since my young lady's going into France, sir, the fool hath much pined away.

Lear
No more of that. Go you and tell my daughter I would speak with her. Call hither my fool. O, you sir, you, come you hither, sir. Who am I, sir?

Oswald
My lady's father.

Lear
My lady's father? My lord's knave, you whoreson dog, you slave, you cur.

Oswald
I am none of these, my lord. I beseech your pardon.

Lear
Do you bandy looks with me, you rascal?

Oswald
I'll not be struck, my lord.

Kent
Nor tripped neither, you base football player.

Lear
I thank thee, fellow. Thou servest me, and I'll love thee.

Kent
Come, sir, arise, away. I'll teach you differences. If you will measure your lubber's length again, tarry. But away, away. Have you wisdom?

Lear
Now, my friendly knave, I thank thee. There's earnest of thy service.

Fool
Let me hire him too.

Lear
How now, my pretty knave?

Fool
Sirrah, you were best take my coxcomb.

Kent
Why, fool?

Fool
Why? For taking one's part that's out of favour. This fellow has banished two of his daughters and did the third a blessing against his will. If thou follow him, thou must needs wear my coxcomb. How now, nuncle, would I had two coxcombs and two daughters.

Lear
Why, my boy?

Fool
If I gave them all my living, I'd keep my coxcombs myself. There's mine. Beg another of thy daughters.

Lear
Take heed, sirrah, the whip.

Fool
Truth's a dog must to kennel.
Sirrah, I'll teach thee a speech.

Lear
Do.

Fool
Mark it nuncle.
Have more than thou showest
Speak less than thou knowest
Lend less than thou owest
Learn more than thou trowest
Set less than thou throwest
Leave thy drink and thy whore
And keep in·a·door
And thou shalt have more
Than two tens to a score.

Kent
This is nothing, fool.

Fool
Then tis like the breath of an unfeed lawyer, you gave me nothing for it. Can you make no use of nothing, nuncle?

Lear
Why, no, boy. Nothing can be made out of nothing.

Fool
Prithee, tell him, so much the rent of his land comes to. He will not believe a fool.

Lear
A bitter fool.

Fool
Dost thou know the difference, my boy, between a bitter fool and a sweet fool?

Lear
No, lad, teach me.

Fool
That lord that counselled thee
To give away thy land
Come place him here by me
Do thou for him stand
The sweet and bitter fool
Will presently appear

The one in motley here
The other found out there.

Lear
Dost thou call me fool, boy?

Fool
All thy other titles thou hast given away. That thou wast
born with.

Kent
This is not altogether fool, my lord.

Fool
Give me an egg, nuncle, and I'll give thee two crowns.

Lear
What two crowns shall they be?

Fool
Why, after I have cut the egg in the middle, and eat up
the meat, the two crowns of the egg. When thou clovest
thy crown in the middle, and gavest away both parts,
thou borest thy ass on thy back over the dirt. Thou
hadst little wit in thy bald crown, when thou gavest thy
golden one away.
Fools had ne'er less wit in a year
For wise men are grown foppish
They know not how their wits to wear
Their manners are so apish.

Lear
When were you wont to be so full of songs, sirrah?

Fool
I have used it, nuncle, ever since thou madest thy
daughters thy mothers.
Then they for sudden joy did weep
And I for sorrow sung
That such a king should play bo·peep
And go the fools among.
Prithee, nuncle, keep a schoolmaster that can teach thy
fool to lie. I would fain learn to lie.

Lear

An you lie, sirrah, we'll have you whipped.

Fool

I marvel what kin thou and thy daughters are. They'll
have me whipped for speaking true, thou'lt have me
whipped for lying. And sometimes I am whipped for
holding my peace. I had rather be any kind of thing than
a fool. And yet I would not be thee, nuncle. Thou hast
pared thy wit on both sides, and left nothing in the
middle. Here comes one of the parings.

Lear

How now daughter? what makes that frontlet on?
Methinks you are too much of late in the frown.

Fool

Thou wast a pretty fellow when thou hadst no need to
care for her frowning. Yes, forsooth, I will hold my tongue,
so your face bids me, though you say nothing.

Goneril

Not only, sir, this your all-licensed fool
But other of your insolent retinue
Do hourly carp and quarrel, breaking forth
In rank and not to be endured riots. Sir
I had thought, by making this well known unto you
To have found a safe redress, but now grow fearful
By what yourself too late have spoke and done
That you protect this course, and put it on
By your allowance, which if you should, the fault
Would not scape censure, nor the redresses sleep.

Lear

Are you our daughter?

Goneril

I would you would make use of that good wisdom
Whereof I know you are fraught and put away
These dispositions that of late transform you
From what you rightly are.

Fool
May not an ass know when the cart draws the horse?

Lear
Doth any here know me? This is not Lear.
Doth Lear walk thus? speak thus? Where are his eyes?
Who is it that can tell me who I am?

Fool
Lear's shadow.

Lear
I would learn that. For by the marks of sovereignty,
knowledge and reason, I should be false persuaded I had
daughters. Your name, fair gentlewoman?

Goneril
This admiration, sir, is much of the savour
Of other your new pranks. I do beseech you
To understand my purposes aright.
As you are old and reverend should be wise.
Here do you keep a hundred knights and squires
Men so disordered, so deboshed and bold
That this our court, infected with their manners
Shows like a riotous inn. Epicurism and lust
Make it more like a tavern or a brothel
Than a graced palace. The shame itself doth speak
For instant remedy. Be then desired
By her that else will take the thing she begs
A little to disquantity your train
And the remainder that shall still depend
To be such men as may besort your age
And know themselves and you.

Lear
                                        Darkness and devils.
Saddle my horses, call my train together.
Degenerate bastard, I'll not trouble thee.
Yet have I left a daughter.

Goneril
You strike my people and your disordered rabble
Make servants of their betters.

Lear
Woe that too late repents. O sir, are you come?
Is it your will? Speak, sir. Prepare my horses.
Ingratitude, thou marble-hearted fiend
More hideous when thou showst thee in a child
Than the sea-monster.

Albany
                    Pray sir, be patient.

Lear
Detested kite, thou liest.
My train are men of choice and rarest parts
That all particulars of duty know
And in the most exact regard support
The worships of their name. O Lear, Lear, Lear
Beat at this gate that let thy folly in
And thy dear judgment out.

Albany
My lord I am guiltless as I am ignorant
Of what hath moved you.

Lear
                    It may be so, my lord.
Hear, Nature, hear. Dear goddess, hear.
Suspend thy purpose if thou didst intend
To make this creature fruitful.
Into her womb convey sterility
Dry up in her the organs of increase
And from her derogate body never spring
A babe to honour her. If she must teem
Create her child of spleen, that it may live
And be a thwart disnatured torment to her.
Let it stamp wrinkles in her brow of youth
With cadent tears fret channels in her cheeks
Turn all her mother's pains and benefits
To laughter and contempt, that she may feel
How sharper than a serpent's tooth it is
To have a thankless child. Away, away.

Albany
Now gods that we adore, whereof comes this?

Goneril
Never afflict yourself to know the cause
But let his disposition have that scope
That dotage gives it.

Lear
What, fifty of my followers at a clap?
Within a fortnight?

Albany
                    What's the matter, sir?

Lear
                                        I'll tell thee.
Life and death, I am ashamed
That thou hast power to shake my manhood thus.
That these hot tears which break from me perforce
Should make thee worth them. Blasts and fogs upon thee.
The untented woundings of a father's curse
Pierce every sense about thee. Old fond eyes
Beweep this cause again I'll pluck ye out.
Yet have I left a daughter
Who I am sure is kind and comfortable.
When she shall hear this of thee, with her nails
She'll flay thy wolvish visage. Thou shalt find
That I'll resume the shape which thou dost think
I have cast off for ever. Thou shalt
I warrant thee.

Goneril
                    Do you mark that, my lord?

Albany
I cannot be so partial, Goneril
To the great love I bear you.

Goneril
Pray you content. What, Oswald, ho.
You sir, more knave than fool, after your master.

Fool
Nuncle Lear, nuncle Lear, tarry and take the fool with thee.

Goneril
Tis politic and safe to let him keep
At point a hundred knights. Yes, that on every dream
Each buzz, each fancy, each complaint, dislike
He may enguard his dotage with their powers
And hold our lives in mercy. Oswald I say.

Albany
Well you may fear too far.

Goneril
      Safer than trust too far
What, have you writ that letter to my sister?

Oswald
Yes, madam.

Goneril
Take you some company and away to horse.
Inform her full of my particular fear
And thereto add such reasons of your own
As may compact it more. Get you gone
And hasten your return. No, no, my lord
This milky gentleness and course of yours
Though I condemn not, yet under pardon
You are much more attasked for want of wisdom
Than praised for harmful mildness.

Albany
How far your eyes may pierce I cannot tell.
Striving to better oft we mar what's well.

Goneril
Nay, then.

Albany
Well, well, the event.

5

Lear
Go you before to Cornwall with these letters. Acquaint my daughter no further with any thing you know than comes from her demand out of the letter. If your diligence be not speedy, I shall be there afore you.

Kent
I will not sleep, my lord, till I have delivered your letter.

Fool
If a man's brains were in his heels, were it not in danger of kibes?

Lear
Ay, boy.

Fool
Then, I prithee, be merry. Thy wit shall never go slipshod.

Lear
Ha, ha, ha.

Fool
Shalt see thy other daughter will use thee kindly. For though she's as like this as a crab's like an apple, yet I can tell what I can tell.

Lear
Why, what canst thou tell, my boy?

Fool
She will taste as like this as a crab does to a crab. Thou canst tell why one's nose stands in the middle of one's face?

Lear
No.

Fool
Why, to keep one's eyes on either side of one's nose, that what a man cannot smell out, he may spy into.

Lear
I did her wrong.

Fool
Canst tell how an oyster makes his shell?

Lear
No.

Fool
Nor I neither. But I can tell why a snail has a house.

Lear
Why?

Fool
Why, to put his head in, not to give it away to his daughters, and leave his horns without a case.

Lear
I will forget my nature. So kind a father. Be my horses ready?

Fool
Thy asses are gone about them. The reason why the seven stars are no more than seven is a pretty reason.

Lear
Because they are not eight?

Fool
Yes, indeed. Thou wouldst make a good fool.

Lear
To take it again perforce. Monster ingratitude.

Fool
If thou wert my fool, nuncle, I'd have thee beaten for being old before thy time.

Lear
How's that?

Fool
Thou shouldst not have been old till thou hadst been wise.

Lear
O let me not be mad, not mad, sweet heaven.
Keep me in temper. I would not be mad.
How now, are the horses ready?

Gentleman
Ready, my lord.

Lear
Come, boy.

6

Edmund
Save thee, Curan.

Curan
And you, sir. I have been with your father and given him
notice that the Duke of Cornwall and Regan his Duchess
will be here with him this night.

Edmund
How comes that?

Curan
Nay, I know not. You have heard of the news abroad?

Edmund
Not I. What are they?

Curan
Have you heard of no likely wars toward twixt the Dukes
of Cornwall and Albany?

Edmund
Not a word.

Curan
You may do, then, in time. Fare you well, sir.

Edmund
The Duke be here tonight? The better, best.
This weaves itself perforce into my business.
Brother a word. Descend, brother I say.

My father watches. O sir, fly this place.
Intelligence is given where you are hid.
Have you not spoken gainst the Duke of Cornwall?
He's coming hither. Now, in the night, in the haste
And Regan with him. Have you nothing said
Upon his party gainst the Duke of Albany?
Advise yourself.

Edgar

      I am sure on it, not a word.

Edmund

I hear my father coming. Pardon me.
In cunning I must draw my sword upon you.
Draw, seem to defend yourself. Now quit you well.
Yield, come before my father. Light ho, here.
Fly brother. Torches, torches. So farewell.
Some blood drawn on me would beget opinion
Of my more fierce endeavour. I have seen drunkards
Do more than this in sport. Father, father.

Gloucester

Now, Edmund, where's the villain?

Edmund

Here stood he in the dark, his sharp sword out
Mumbling of wicked charms, conjuring the moon
To stand auspicious mistress.

Gloucester

But where is he?

Edmund

Look, sir, I bleed.

Gloucester

Where is the villain, Edmund?

Edmund

Fled this way, sir. When by no means he could.

Gloucester

Pursue him, ho. Go after. By no means what?

Edmund
Persuade me to the murder of your lordship.
But that I told him the revenging gods
Gainst parricides did all their thunders bend.
With his prepared sword, he charges home
My unprovided body, lanced mine arm.
But when he saw my best alarumed spirits
Bold in the quarrel's right, roused to the encounter
Full suddenly he fled.

Gloucester
$\qquad\qquad$ Let him fly far.
Not in this land shall he remain uncaught
And found dispatch. The noble Duke my master
My worthy arch and patron, comes tonight.
By his authority I will proclaim it
That he which finds him shall deserve our thanks
Bringing the murderous coward to the stake.
He that conceals him, death.
All ports I'll bar. The villain shall not scape.
The Duke must grant me that. Besides, his picture
I will send far and near, that all the kingdom
May have due note of him. And of my land
Loyal and natural boy, I'll work the means
To make thee capable.

Cornwall
How now, my noble friend. Since I came hither
Which I can call but now, I have heard strange news.

Regan
If it be true, all vengeance comes too short
Which can pursue the offender. How dost, my lord?

Gloucester
O, madam, my old heart is cracked, it's cracked.

Regan
What, did my father's godson seek your life?
He whom my father named your Edgar?

Gloucester
O, lady, lady, shame would have it hid.

Regan
Was he not companion with the riotous knights
That tend upon my father?

Gloucester
I know not, madam. Tis too bad, too bad.

Edmund
Yes, madam, he was of that consort.

Regan
No marvel, then, though he were ill affected.
I have this present evening from my sister
Been well informed of them and with such cautions
That if they come to sojourn at my house
I'll not be there.

Cornwall
                    Nor I, I assure thee, Regan.
Edmund, I hear that you have shown your father
A childlike office.

Edmund
                    Twas my duty, sir.

Gloucester
He did bewray his practise and received
This hurt you see striving to apprehend him.

Cornwall
Is he pursued?

Gloucester
                    Ay, my good lord.

Cornwall
If he be taken he shall never more
Be feared of doing harm. For you Edmund
Whose virtue and obedience doth this instant
So much commend itself, you shall be ours.
Natures of such deep trust we shall much need.
You we first seize on.

Edmund

                      I shall serve you, sir
Truly, however else.

Gloucester

               For him I thank your Grace.

Cornwall

You know not why we came to visit you.

Regan

Thus out of season, threading dark-eyed night.
Occasions, noble Gloucester, of some poise
Wherein we must have use of your advice.
Our good old friend
Lay comforts to your bosom and bestow
Your needful counsel to our business
Which craves the instant use.

Gloucester

                   I serve you madam.
Your Graces are right welcome.

7

Oswald

Good dawning to thee, friend. Art of this house?

Kent

Ay.

Oswald

Where may we set our horses?

Kent

In the mire.

Oswald

Prithee, if thou lovest me, tell me.

Kent

I love thee not.

Oswald
Why dost thou use me thus? I know thee not.

Kent
Fellow, I know thee.

Oswald
What dost thou know me for?

Kent
A knave, a base, proud, shallow, beggarly knave. One that wouldst be a bawd, in way of good service, and art nothing but the composition of a knave, beggar, coward, pandar, and the son and heir of a mongrel bitch. One whom I will beat into clamorous whining, if thou deniest the least syllable of thy addition.

Oswald
Why, what a monstrous fellow art thou, thus to rail on one that is neither known of thee nor knows thee.

Kent
What a brazen-faced varlet art thou to deny thou knowest me. Is it two days ago since I tripped up thy heels, and beat thee before the King? Draw, you rogue. For though it be night, yet the moon shines. Draw, you whoreson cullionly barber-monger, draw.

Oswald
Away. I have nothing to do with thee.

Kent
Draw, you rascal. You come with letters against the King. Draw, you rogue, or I'll so carbonado your shanks. Draw, you rascal.

Oswald
Help, ho, murder, help.

Kent
Strike, you slave. Stand, rogue, stand, you neat slave, strike.

Oswald
Help, ho. Murder, murder.

Edmund
How now. What's the matter?

Kent
With you, goodman boy, an you please. Come, I'll flesh ye. Come on, young master.

Gloucester
Weapons, arms. What's the matter here?

Cornwall
Keep peace, upon your lives. He dies that strikes again. What is the matter?

Regan
The messengers from our sister and the King.

Cornwall
What is your difference? Speak.

Oswald
I am scarce in breath, my lord.

Kent
No marvel, you have so bestirred your valour. You cowardly rascal, nature disclaims thee. A tailor made thee.

Cornwall
Thou art a strange fellow. A tailor make a man?

Kent
Ay, a tailor, sir. A stonecutter or painter could not have made him so ill, though he had been but two hours at the trade.

Cornwall
Speak yet, how grew your quarrel?

Oswald
This ancient ruffian, sir, whose life I have spared at suit of his gray beard.

Kent
Thou whoreson zed, thou unnecessary letter. My lord, if
you will give me leave, I will tread this unbolted villain
into mortar, and daub the wall of a jakes with him. Spare
my gray beard, you wagtail?

Cornwall
Peace, sirrah. Know you no reverence?

Kent
Yes, sir. But anger hath a privilege.

Cornwall
Why art thou angry?

Kent
That such a slave as this should wear a sword
Who wears no honesty.
A plague upon your epileptic visage.
Smile you my speeches as I were a fool?
Goose, if I had you upon Sarum plain,
I'd drive ye cackling home to Camelot.

Cornwall
Why, art thou mad, old fellow?

Gloucester
How fell you out? Say that.

Kent
No contraries hold more antipathy
Than I and such a knave.

Cornwall
What's his offence?

Kent
His countenance likes me not.

Cornwall
No more, perchance, does mine, nor his, nor hers.

Kent
Sir, tis my occupation to be plain.
I have seen better faces in my time

Than stands on any shoulder that I see
Before me at this instant.

Cornwall
                        This is some fellow
Who having been praised for bluntness doth affect
A saucy roughness and constrains the garb
Quite from his nature. He cannot flatter, he
An honest mind and plain, he must speak truth.

Kent
Sir, in good sooth, in sincere verity
Under the allowance of your great aspect
Whose influence, like the wreath of radiant fire
On flickering Phoebus front –

Cornwall
What meanst by this?

Kent
To go out of my dialect, which you discommend so much.

Cornwall
What was the offence you gave him?

Oswald
I never gave him any.
It pleased the King his master very late
To strike at me, upon his misconstruction.
When he, conjunct and flattering his displeasure
Tripped me behind, got praises of the King
And in the fleshment of this dread exploit
Drew on me here again.

Cornwall
                        Fetch forth the stocks.
You stubborn ancient knave, you reverend braggart
We'll teach you.

Kent
                    Sir, I am too old to learn.
Call not your stocks for me, I serve the King
On whose employment I was sent to you.

Cornwall
Fetch forth the stocks. As I have life and honour
There shall he sit till noon.

Regan
Till noon? Till night, my lord, and all night too.

Kent
Why, madam, if I were your father's dog
You should not use me so.

Regan
                              Sir, being his knave, I will.

Cornwall
This is a fellow of the self-same colour
Our sister speaks of. Come, bring away the stocks.

Gloucester
Let me beseech your grace not to do so.
The King must take it ill
That he's so slightly valued in his messenger
Should have him thus restrained.

Cornwall
I'll answer that.

Regan
My sister may receive it much more worse
To have her gentleman abused, assaulted
For following her affairs. Put in his legs.
Come my good lord, away.

Gloucester
I am sorry for thee friend. Tis the Duke's pleasure
Whose disposition, all the world well knows
Will not be rubbed nor stopped. I'll entreat for thee.

Kent
Pray do not sir. I have watched and travelled hard.
Some time I shall sleep out. The rest I'll whistle.
A good man's fortune may grow out at heels.
Give you good morrow.

Gloucester
The Duke's to blame in this. Twill be ill taken.

Kent
Approach thou beacon to this under globe
That by thy comfortable beams I may
Peruse this letter. Tis from Cordelia
Who hath most fortunately been informed
Of my obscured course.
Fortune, good night. Smile once more, turn thy wheel.

8

Edgar
I heard myself proclaimed
And by the happy hollow of a tree
Escaped the hunt. No port is free, no place
That guard and most unusual vigilance
Does not attend my taking. Whiles I may scape
I will preserve myself, and am bethought
To take the basest and most poorest shape
That ever penury, in contempt of man
Brought near to beast. My face I'll grime with filth
Blanket my loins, elf all my hair in knots
And with presented nakedness outface
The winds and persecutions of the sky.
The country gives me proof and precedent
Of Bedlam beggars, who with roaring voices
Strike in their numbed and mortified bare arms
Pins, wooden pricks, nails, sprigs of rosemary.
And with this horrible object, from low farms
Poor pelting villages, sheepcotes and mills
Sometime with lunatic bans, sometime with prayers
Enforce their charity. Poor Turlygod, poor Tom.
That's something yet. Edgar I nothing am.

9

Lear
Tis strange that they should so depart from home
And not send back my messenger.

Kent
Hail to thee, noble master.

Lear
Ha. Makest thou this shame thy pastime?

Kent
No, my lord.

Fool
Ha, ha. He wears cruel garters. Horses are tied by the
heads, dogs and bears by the neck, monkeys by the
loins, and men by the legs.

Lear
What's he that hath so much thy place mistook
To set thee here?

Kent
It is both he and she.
Your son and daughter.

Lear
No.

Kent
Yes.

Lear
No, I say.

Kent
I say, yea.

Lear
No, no, they would not.

Kent
Yes, they have.

Lear
By Jupiter, I swear, no.

Kent
By Juno, I swear, ay.

Lear
They durst not do it
They could not, would not do it. Tis worse than murder
To do upon respect such violent outrage.
Resolve me, with all modest haste, which way
Thou mightst deserve, or they impose, this usage
Coming from us.

Kent
               My lord, when at their home
I did commend your highness letters to them
Ere I was risen from the place that showed
My duty kneeling, came there a reeking post
From Goneril, his mistress salutations
Delivered letters, spite of intermission
Which presently they read, on whose contents
They summoned up their meiny, straight took horse
Commanded me to follow, and attend
The leisure of their answer, gave me cold looks
And meeting here the other messenger
Whose welcome, I perceived, had poisoned mine
Having more man than wit about me, drew.
He raised the house with loud and coward cries.
Your son and daughter found this trespass worth
The shame which here it suffers.

Fool
Winter's not gone yet, if the wild-geese fly that way.

Lear
O how this mother swells up toward my heart.
Hysterica passio, down, thou climbing sorrow
Thy element's below. Where is this daughter?

Kent
With the Earl, sir, here within.

Lear
Follow me not. Stay here.

Gentleman
Made you no more offence but what you speak of?

Kent
No. How chance the King comes with so small a train?

Fool
And thou hadst been set in the stocks for that question, thou hadst well deserved it.

Kent
Why, fool?

Fool
We'll set thee to school to an ant, to teach thee there's no labouring in the winter. All that follow their noses are led by their eyes but blind men, and there's not a nose among twenty but can smell him that's stinking. When a wise man gives thee better counsel, give me mine again. I would have none but knaves follow it, since a fool gives it.

Kent
Where learned you this, fool?

Fool
Not in the stocks, fool.

Lear
Deny to speak with me? they are sick? they are weary?
They have travelled all the night? Mere fetches.
The images of revolt and flying off.
Fetch me a better answer.

Gloucester
                    My dear lord
You know the fiery quality of the Duke
How unremoveable and fixed he is
In his own course.

Lear
Vengeance, plague, death, confusion.
Fiery? what quality? Why, Gloucester, Gloucester
I'd speak with the Duke of Cornwall and his wife.

Gloucester
Well, my good lord, I have informed them so.

Lear
Informed them? Dost thou understand me, man?

Gloucester
Ay, my good lord.

Lear
The King would speak with Cornwall. The dear father
Would with his daughter speak, commands her service.
Are they informed of this? My breath and blood.
Fiery? The fiery Duke? Tell the hot Duke that –
No, but not yet. Maybe he is not well
Infirmity doth still neglect all office
Whereto our health is bound. We are not ourselves
When nature, being oppressed, commands the mind
To suffer with the body. I'll forbear
And am fallen out with my more headier will
To take the indisposed and sickly fit
For the sound man. Death on my state, wherefore
Should he sit here? Give me my servant forth.
Go tell the Duke and's wife I'd speak with them.
Now, presently, bid them come forth and hear me
Or at their chamberdoor I'll beat the drum
Till it cry sleep to death.

Gloucester
I would have all well betwixt you.

Lear
O me, my heart, my rising heart, but, down.

Fool
Cry to it, nuncle, as the cockney did to the eels when
she put 'em in the pastry alive. She knapped 'em on the
coxcombs with a stick, and cried 'down, wantons, down.'

Lear
Good morrow to you both.

Cornwall
Hail to your grace.

Regan
I am glad to see your highness.

Lear
Regan I think you are. I know what reason
I have to think so. If thou shouldst not be glad
I would divorce me from thy mother's tomb
Sepulchring an adultress. O are you free?
Some other time for that. Beloved Regan
Thy sister's naught. O Regan, she hath tied
Sharp toothed unkindness like a vulture here.
I can scarce speak to thee. Thou'lt not believe
With how depraved a quality. O Regan.

Regan
I pray you sir, take patience. I have hope
You less know how to value her desert
Than she to scant her duty.

Lear
                              Say, how is that?

Regan
I cannot think my sister in the least
Would fail her obligation. If sir, perchance
She have restrained the riots of your followers
Tis on such ground, and to such wholesome end
As clears her from all blame.

Lear
                              My curses on her.

Regan
O sir, you are old.
Nature in you stands on the very verge
Of her confine. You should be ruled and led
By some discretion that discerns your state

Better than you yourself. Therefore I pray you
That to our sister you do make return.
Say you have wronged her sir.

Lear

                                  Ask her forgiveness?
Do you but mark how this becomes the house?
'Dear daughter, I confess that I am old.
Age is unnecessary. On my knees I beg
That you'll vouchsafe me raiment, bed, and food.'

Regan

Good sir, no more. These are unsightly tricks.
Return you to my sister.

Lear

                               Never Regan.
She hath abated me of half my train
Looked black upon me, struck me with her tongue
Most serpent-like, upon the very heart.
All the stored vengeances of heaven fall
On her ingrateful top. Strike her young bones
You taking airs with lameness.

Cornwall

                               Fie, sir, fie.

Lear

You nimble lightnings, dart your blinding flames
Into her scornful eyes. Infect her beauty
You fen-sucked fogs, drawn by the powerful sun
To fall and blast her pride.

Regan

O the blest gods. So will you wish on me
When the rash mood is on.

Lear

No Regan, thou shalt never have my curse.
Thy tender hefted nature shall not give
Thee over to harshness. Her eyes are fierce but thine
Do comfort and not burn. Thou better knowst

The offices of nature, bond of childhood
Effects of courtesy, dues of gratitude.
Thy half of the kingdom hast thou not forgot
Wherein I thee endowed.

Regan

                Good sir, to the purpose.

Lear

Who put my man in the stocks?

Cornwall

                What trumpet's that?

Regan

I know it, my sister's. This approves her letter
That she would soon be here. Is your lady come?

Lear

This is a slave, whose easy-borrowed pride
Dwells in the fickle grace of her he follows.
Out, varlet, from my sight.

Cornwall

                What means your grace?

Lear

Who stocked my servant? Regan, I have good hope
Thou didst not know on't. Who comes here? O heavens
If you do love old men, if your sweet sway
Allow obedience, if you yourselves are old
Make it your cause. Send down and take my part.
Art not ashamed to look upon this beard?
O Regan, wilt thou take her by the hand?

Goneril

Why not by the hand, sir? How have I offended?
All's not offence that indiscretion finds
And dotage terms so.

Lear

              O sides, you are too tough
Will you yet hold? How came my man in the stocks?

Cornwall
I set him there sir, but his own disorders
Deserved much less advancement.

Lear
You? Did you?

Regan
I pray you father, being weak, seem so.
If till the expiration of your month
You will return and sojourn with my sister
Dismissing half your train, come then to me.
I am now from home, and out of that provision
Which shall be needful for your entertainment.

Lear
Return to her and fifty men dismissed?
No, rather I abjure all roofs and choose
To wage against the enmity of the air
To be a comrade with the wolf and owl
Necessity's sharp pinch. Return with her?
Persuade me rather to be slave and sumpter
To this detested groom.

Goneril
At your choice, sir.

Lear
I prithee, daughter, do not make me mad.
I will not trouble thee, my child, farewell.
We'll no more meet, no more see one another.
But yet thou art my flesh, my blood, my daughter
Or rather a disease that's in my flesh
Which I must needs call mine. Thou art a boil
A plague sore, an embossed carbuncle
In my corrupted blood. But I'll not chide thee
Mend when thou canst. Be better at thy leisure.
I can be patient. I can stay with Regan
I and my hundred knights.

Regan
                          Not altogether so.
I looked not for you yet nor am provided
For your fit welcome. Give ear sir to my sister
For those that mingle reason with your passion
Must be content to think you old.
But she knows what she does.

Lear
                          Is this well spoken?

Regan
I dare avouch it, sir. What, fifty followers?
Is it not well? What should you need of more?
Yea, or so many, since that both charge and danger
Speak gainst so great a number? How in one house
Should many people under two commands
Hold amity? Tis hard, almost impossible.

Goneril
Why might not you, my lord, receive attendance
From those that she calls servants or from mine?

Regan
Why not, my lord? If then they chanced to slack you
We could control them. If you will come to me
For now I spy a danger, I entreat you
To bring but five and twenty. To no more
Will I give place or notice.

Lear
I gave you all.

Regan
                          And in good time you gave it.

Lear
Made you my guardians, my depositaries
But kept a reservation to be followed
With such a number. What, must I come to you
With five and twenty? Regan, said you so?

Regan
And speak it again, my lord. No more with me.

Lear
Those wicked creatures yet do look well·favoured
When others are more wicked. Not being the worst
Stands in some rank of praise. I'll go with thee.
Thy fifty yet doth double five and twenty
And thou art twice her love.

Goneril
                              Hear me, my lord.
What need you five and twenty, ten, or five
To follow in a house where twice so many
Have a command to tend you?

Regan
                              What need one?

Lear
O reason not the need. Our basest beggars
Are in the poorest thing superfluous.
Allow not nature more than nature needs
Man's life's as cheap as beast's. Thou art a lady.
If only to go warm were gorgeous
Why nature needs not what thou gorgeous wear'st
Which scarcely keeps thee warm. But for true need.
You heavens give me that patience, patience I need
You see me here, you gods, a poor old man
As full of grief as age, wretched in both.
If it be you that stir these daughters hearts
Against their father, fool me not so much
To bear it tamely. Touch me with noble anger
And let not women's weapons, water·drops
Stain my man's cheeks. No, you unnatural hags
I will have such revenges on you both
That all the world shall – I will do such things
What they are, yet I know not, but they shall be
The terrors of the earth. You think I'll weep.
No, I'll not weep.

I have full cause of weeping, but this heart
Shall break into a hundred thousand flaws
Or ere I'll weep. O fool, I shall go mad.

Cornwall
Let us withdraw. Twill be a storm.

Regan
This house is little. The old man and's people
Cannot be well bestowed.

Goneril
Tis his own blame. Hath put himself from rest
And must needs taste his folly.

Regan
For his particular I'll receive him gladly
But not one follower.

Goneril
                So am I purposed.
Where is my lord of Gloucester?

Cornwall
Followed the old man forth. He is returned.

Gloucester
The King is in high rage.

Cornwall
                Whither is he going?

Gloucester
He calls to horse, but will I know not whither.

Cornwall
Tis best to give him way. He leads himself.

Goneril
My lord, entreat him by no means to stay.

Gloucester
Alack, the night comes on and the bleak winds
Do sorely ruffle. For many miles about
There's scarce a bush.

Regan

                                O sir, to wilful men
The injuries that they themselves procure
Must be their schoolmasters. Shut up your doors.
He is attended with a desperate train
And what they may incense him to, being apt
To have his ear abused, wisdom bids fear.

Cornwall

Shut up your doors, my lord. Tis a wild night
My Regan counsels well. Come out of the storm.

INTERVAL

10

Kent
Who's there, besides foul weather?

Gentleman
One minded like the weather, most unquietly.

Kent
I know you. Where's the King?

Gentleman
Contending with the fretful element.
Bids the wind blow the earth into the sea
Or swell the curled water bove the main
That things might change or cease.
Unbonnetted he runs and bids
What will, take all.

Kent
                    But who is with him?

Gentleman
None but the Fool, who labours to out-jest
His heart-struck injuries.

Kent
                         Sir, I do know you
And dare upon the warrant of my note
Commend a dear thing to you.
From France there comes a power
Into this scattered kingdom, who already
Wise in our negligence, have secret feet
In some of our best ports, and are at point
To show their open banner. Now to you.
If on my credit you dare build so far
To make your speed to Dover, you shall find
Some that will thank you, making just report
Of how unnatural and bemadding sorrow
The King hath cause to plain.
If you shall see Cordelia

As fear not but you shall, show her this ring
And she will tell you who your fellow is
That yet you do not know. Fie on this storm.
I will go seek the King.

11

Lear
Blow winds and crack your cheeks. Rage, blow.
You cataracts and hurricanoes, spout
Till you have drenched our steeples, drowned the cocks.
You sulphurous and thought executing fires
Vaunt-couriers to oak cleaving thunderbolts
Singe my white head. And thou all shaking thunder
Smite flat the thick rotundity of the world.
Crack nature's moulds, all germens spill at once
That make ingrateful man.

Fool
O nuncle, court holy water in a dry house is better than
this rain-water out of door. Good nuncle, in, and ask thy
daughters blessing. Here's a night pities neither wise
man nor fool.

Lear
Rumble thy bellyful. Spit, fire, spout, rain.
Nor rain, wind, thunder, fire, are my daughters.
I tax not you, you elements, with unkindness.
I never gave you kingdom, called you children
You owe me no subscription. Then let fall
Your horrible pleasure. Here I stand, your slave
A poor, infirm, weak, and despised old man
But yet I call you servile ministers
That have with two pernicious daughters joined
Your high engendered battles gainst a head
So old and white as this. O, O, tis foul.

Fool
He that has a house to put his head in has a good head-piece.

Lear
No, I will be the pattern of all patience.
I will say nothing.

Kent
Alas, sir, are you here?

Lear
                              Let the great gods
That keep this dreadful pother o'er our heads
Find out their enemies now. Tremble thou wretch
That hast within thee undivulged crimes
Unwhipped of justice. Hide thee thou bloody hand
Thou perjured and thou simular of virtue
That art incestuous. I am a man
More sinned against than sinning.

Kent
                                        Alack, bare headed.
Gracious my lord, hard by here is a hovel
Some friendship will it lend you gainst the tempest.
Repose you there.

Lear
                    My wits begin to turn.
Come on my boy. How dost, my boy? Art cold?
I am cold myself. Where is this straw, my fellow?
The art of our necessities is strange
That can make vile things precious. Come, your hovel.
Poor fool and knave, I have one part in my heart
That's sorry yet for thee.

Fool
He that has and a little tiny wit
With hey, ho, the wind and the rain
Must make content with his fortunes fit
For the rain it raineth every day.

Lear
True, my good boy. Come, bring us to this hovel.

12

Gloucester
Edmund, I like not this unnatural dealing. When I desired their leave that I might pity him, they took from me the use of mine own house, charged me, on pain of their perpetual displeasure, neither to speak of him, entreat for him, nor any way sustain him.

Edmund
Most savage and unnatural.

Gloucester
Go to, say you nothing. There's a division betwixt the dukes, and a worse matter than that. I have received a letter this night. Tis dangerous to be spoken. I have locked the letter in my closet. These injuries the King now bears will be revenged home. There's part of a power already footed. We must incline to the King. I will seek him, and privily relieve him. Go you and maintain talk with the Duke, that my charity be not of him perceived. If he ask for me, I am ill and gone to bed. Though I die for it, as no less is threatened me, the King my old master must be relieved. There is some strange thing toward, Edmund. Pray you, be careful.

Edmund
This courtesy, forbid thee, shall the Duke
Instantly know, and of that letter too.
This seems a fair deserving and must draw me
That which my father loses, no less than all.
The younger rises when the old doth fall.

13

Kent
Here is the place, my lord. Good my lord, enter.

Lear
Let me alone.

Kent
Good my lord, enter here.

Lear
Wilt break my heart?

Kent
I had rather break mine own. Good my lord, enter.

Lear
Thou thinkst tis much that this contentious storm
Invades us to the skin. So tis to thee.
But where the greater malady is fixed
The lesser is scarce felt. This tempest in my mind
Doth from my senses take all feeling else
Save what beats there. Filial ingratitude.
In such a night
To shut me out. Pour on, I will endure.
In such a night as this? O Regan, Goneril
Your old kind father, whose frank heart gave all.
O that way madness lies. Let me shun that.
No more of that.

Kent
                    Good my lord, enter here.

Lear
Prithee, go in thyself, seek thine own ease.
This tempest will not give me leave to ponder
On things would hurt me more. But I'll go in.
In, boy, go first. You houseless poverty
Nay, get thee in. I'll pray and then I'll sleep.
Poor naked wretches, whereso'er you are
That bide the pelting of this pitiless storm
How shall your houseless heads and unfed sides
Your looped and windowed raggedness, defend you
From seasons such as these? O I have ta'en
Too little care of this. Take physic, pomp
Expose thyself to feel what wretches feel
That thou mayst shake the superflux to them
And show the heavens more just.

Edgar
Fathom and half, fathom and half, poor Tom.

Fool
Come not in here, nuncle, here's a spirit.

Kent
Who's there?

Fool
A spirit, a spirit. He says his name's poor Tom.

Kent
What art thou that dost grumble there in the straw?
Come forth.

Edgar
　　　　　Away, the foul fiend follows me.
Through the sharp hawthorn blows the cold wind.

Lear
Hast thou given all to thy two daughters?
And art thou come to this?

Edgar
Who gives any thing to poor Tom? whom the foul fiend
hath led through fire and through flame, and through ford
and whirlipool, o'er bog and quagmire? Do poor Tom
some charity.

Lear
What, have his daughters brought him to this pass?
Couldst thou save nothing? Didst thou give them all?

Fool
Nay, he reserved a blanket, else we had been all
shamed.

Lear
Now all the plagues that in the pendulous air
Hang fated o'er men's faults, light on thy daughters.

Kent
He hath no daughters, sir.

Lear
Death traitor. Nothing could have subdued nature
To such a lowness but his unkind daughters.
Is it the fashion that discarded fathers
Should have thus little mercy on their flesh?
Judicious punishment. Twas this flesh begot
Those pelican daughters.

Edgar
Pillicock sat on Pillicock hill
Halloo, halloo.

Fool
This cold night will turn us all to fools and madmen.

Edgar
Take heed of the foul fiend, obey thy parents, keep thy
word justly, swear not, commit not with man's sworn
spouse, set not thy sweet heart on proud array. Tom's
a-cold.

Lear
What hast thou been?

Edgar
A serving man, proud in heart and mind, that curled my
hair, wore gloves in my cap, served the lust of my
mistress heart, and did the act of darkness with her.
One that slept in the contriving of lust, and waked to do
it. Wine loved I deeply, dice dearly, and in woman out
paramoured the Turk. False of heart, light of ear, bloody
of hand, hog in sloth, fox in stealth, wolf in greediness,
dog in madness, lion in prey. Still through the hawthorn
blows the cold wind.

Lear
Why, thou wert better in thy grave than to answer with
thy uncovered body this extremity of the skies. Is man
no more than this? Consider him well. Thou owest the
worm no silk, the beast no hide, the sheep no wool, the
cat no perfume. Ha, here's three of us are sophisticated.
Thou art the thing itself. Unaccommodated man is no

more but such a poor, bare, forked animal as thou art.
Off, off, you lendings. Come unbutton here.

Fool

Prithee, nuncle, be contented. Tis a naughty night to
swim in. Look, here comes a walking fire.

Edgar

This is the foul fiend Flibbertigibbet. He begins at curfew
and walks till the first cock.

Kent

How fares your grace?

Lear

What's he?

Kent

Who's there? What is it you seek?

Gloucester

What are you there? Your names?

Edgar

Poor Tom. That eats the swimming frog, the toad, the
tadpole, the wall-newt and the water. When the foul fiend
rages, eats cow-dung for sallets, drinks the green mantle
of the standing pool, who is whipped from tithing to tithing.
But mice and rats and such small deer
Have been Tom's food for seven long year.
Peace, Smulkin. Peace, thou fiend.

Gloucester

What, hath your grace no better company?

Edgar

The prince of darkness is a gentleman.

Gloucester

Our flesh and blood is grown so vile, my lord.
That it doth hate what gets it.

Edgar

Poor Tom's a-cold.

Gloucester
Go in with me. My duty cannot suffer
To obey in all your daughters hard commands.
Though their injunction be to bar my doors
And let this tyrannous night take hold upon you
Yet have I ventured to come seek you out
And bring you where both fire and food is ready.

Lear
First let me talk with this philosopher.
What is the cause of thunder?

Kent
Good my lord, take his offer. Go into the house.

Lear
I'll talk a word with this same learned Theban.
What is your study?

Edgar
How to prevent the fiend and to kill vermin.

Lear
Let me ask you one word in private.

Kent
Importune him once more to go my lord.
His wits begin to unsettle.

Gloucester   Canst thou blame him?
His daughters seek his death. Ah, that good Kent.
He said it would be thus, poor banished man.
Thou sayst the King grows mad. I'll tell thee, friend
I am almost mad myself. I had a son
Now outlawed from my blood. He sought my life
But lately, very late. I loved him, friend
No father his son dearer. Truth to tell thee
The grief hath crazed my wits. What a night's this.
I do beseech your Grace.

Lear   O cry your mercy, sir.
Noble philosopher, your company.

Edgar
Tom's a-cold.

Gloucester
In, fellow, there, into the hovel. Keep thee warm.

Lear
Come let's in all.

Kent
                    This way, my lord.

Lear
                                    With him.
I will keep still with my philosopher.

Kent
Good my lord, soothe him. Let him take the fellow.

Gloucester
Take him you on.

Kent
Sirrah, come on. Go along with us.

Lear
Come, good Athenian.

Gloucester
No words, no words. Hush.

Edgar
Child Rowland to the dark tower came
His word was still fie, foh, and fum
I smell the blood of a British man.

14

Cornwall
I will have my revenge ere I depart his house.

Edmund
How, my lord, I may be censured, that nature thus gives
way to loyalty, something fears me to think of.

Cornwall
I now perceive, it was not altogether your brother's evil disposition made him seek his death, but a provoking merit, set a-work by a reprovable badness in himself.

Edmund
How malicious is my fortune, that I must repent to be just. This is the letter he spoke of, which approves him an intelligent party to the advantages of France. O heavens, that this treason were not, or not I the detector.

Cornwall
Go with me to the Duchess.

Edmund
If the matter of this paper be certain, you have mighty business in hand.

Cornwall
True or false, it hath made thee Earl of Gloucester. Seek out where thy father is, that he may be ready for our apprehension.

Edmund
I will persever in my course of loyalty, though the conflict be sore between that and my blood.

Cornwall
I will lay trust upon thee, and thou shalt find a dearer father in my love.

15

Gloucester
Here is better than the open air. Take it thankfully. I will piece out the comfort with what addition I can. I will not be long from you.

Kent
The gods reward your kindness.

Lear
To have a thousand with red burning spits
Come hissing in upon them.

Edgar

The foul fiend bites my back.

Fool

He's mad that trusts in the tameness of a wolf, a horse's health, a boy's love, or a whore's oath.

Lear

It shall be done. I will arraign them straight.
Come, sit thou here, most learned justicer.
Thou, sapient sir, sit here. Now, you she foxes.

Edgar

Come over the bourn, Bessy, to me.

Fool

Her boat hath a leak
And she must not speak
Why she dares not come over to thee.

Edgar

The foul fiend haunts poor Tom in the voice of a nightingale. Croak not, black angel, I have no food for thee.

Kent

How do you sir? Stand you not so amazed.
Will you lie down and rest upon the cushions?

Lear

I'll see their trial first. Bring in the evidence.
Thou robed man of justice, take thy place.
And thou his yoke-fellow of equity
Bench by his side. You are of the commission
Sit you too.

Edgar

Let us deal justly.

Lear

Arraign her first. Tis Goneril. I here take my oath before this honourable assembly, she kicked the poor King her father.

Fool
Come hither, mistress. Is your name Goneril?

Lear
She cannot deny it.

Fool
Cry you mercy, I took you for a joint-stool.

Lear
And here's another, whose warped looks proclaim
What store her heart is made on. Stop her there.
Arms, arms, sword, fire. Corruption in the place.
False justicer, why hast thou let her scape?

Edgar
Bless thy five wits.

Kent
O pity, sir, where is the patience now
That thou so oft have boasted to retain?

Edgar
My tears begin to take his part so much
They'll mar my counterfeiting.

Lear
The little dogs and all, Tray, Blanch, and
Sweet-heart, see, they bark at me.

Edgar
Tom will throw his head at them. Avaunt, you curs.

Lear
Then let them anatomize Regan. See what breeds about
her heart. Is there any cause in nature that makes these
hard hearts? You, sir, I entertain for one of my hundred,
only I do not like the fashion of your garments. You will
say they are Persian attire. But let them be changed.

Kent
Now, good my lord, lie here and rest awhile.

Lear
Make no noise, make no noise. Draw the curtains: so, so, so. We'll go to supper in the morning.

Fool
And I'll go to bed at noon.

Gloucester
Come hither, friend. Where is the King my master?

Kent
Here, sir, but trouble him not, his wits are gone.

Gloucester
Good friend, I prithee take him in thy arms.
I have o'erheard a plot of death upon him.
There is a litter ready, lay him in it
And drive towards Dover, friend, where thou shalt meet
Both welcome and protection. Take up thy master.
If thou shouldst dally half an hour, his life
With thine, and all that offer to defend him
Stand in assured loss. Take up, take up
And follow me, that will to some provision
Give thee quick conduct.

Kent
                              Oppressed nature sleeps.
This rest might yet have balmed thy broken sinews
Which if convenience will not allow
Stand in hard cure. Come, help to bear thy master.
Thou must not stay behind.

Gloucester
                              Come, come away.

Edgar
When we our betters see bearing our woes
We scarcely think our miseries our foes.
How light and portable my pain seems now
When that which makes me bend makes the King bow.
What will hap more tonight, safe scape the King.

16

Cornwall
Post speedily to my lord your husband. Show him this
letter. The army of France is landed. Seek out the traitor
Gloucester.

Regan
Hang him instantly.

Goneril
Pluck out his eyes.

Cornwall
Leave him to my displeasure. Edmund, keep you our
sister company. The revenges we are bound to take upon
your traitorous father are not fit for your beholding.
Farewell, dear sister. Farewell, my lord of Gloucester.
How now, where's the King?

Oswald
My lord of Gloucester hath conveyed him hence.
Some five or six and thirty of his knights
Are gone with him towards Dover, where they boast
To have well armed friends.

Cornwall
Get horses for your mistress.

Goneril
Farewell, sweet lord, and sister.

Cornwall
Edmund, farewell. Go seek the traitor Gloucester.
Pinion him like a thief. Bring him before us.
Though well we may not pass upon his life
Without the form of justice, yet our power
Shall do a courtesy to our wrath, which men
May blame but not control. Who's there, the traitor?

Regan
Ingrateful fox. Tis he.

Cornwall
Bind fast his corky arms.

Gloucester
What mean your graces?
Good my friends, consider. You are my guests.
Do me no foul play, friends.

Cornwall
Bind him, I say.

Regan
Hard, hard. O filthy traitor.

Gloucester
Unmerciful lady as you are, I'm none.

Cornwall
To this chair bind him. Villain, thou shalt find –

Gloucester
By the kind gods, tis most ignobly done
To pluck me by the beard.

Regan
So white, and such a traitor.

Gloucester
Wicked lady
These hairs which thou dost ravish from my chin
Will quicken and accuse thee. I am your host.
With robbers hands my hospitable favours
You should not ruffle thus. What will you do?

Cornwall
Come, sir. What letters had you late from France?

Regan
Be simple, answerer. For we know the truth.

Cornwall
And what confederacy have you with the traitors
Late footed in the kingdom?

Regan
To whose hands have you sent the lunatic King? Speak.

Gloucester
I have a letter guessingly set down
Which came from one that's of a neutral heart
And not from one opposed.

Cornwall
Cunning.

Regan
       And false.

Cornwall
Where hast thou sent the King?

Gloucester
                  To Dover.

Regan
Wherefore to Dover? Wast thou not charged at peril –

Cornwall
Wherefore to Dover? Let him first answer that.

Gloucester
I am tied to the stake and I must stand the course.

Regan
Wherefore to Dover?

Gloucester
Because I would not see thy cruel nails
Pluck out his poor old eyes, nor thy fierce sister
In his anointed flesh rash boarish fangs.
The sea, with such a storm as his bare head
In hell-black night endured, would have buoyed up
And quenched the stelled fires.
Yet poor old heart, he holp the heavens to rain.
If wolves had at thy gate howled that dern time
Thou shouldst have said 'Good porter, turn the key
All cruels else subscribe'. But I shall see
The winged Vengeance overtake such children.

Cornwall
See it shalt thou never. Fellows, hold the chair.
Upon these eyes of thine I'll set my foot.

Gloucester
He that will think to live till he be old
Give me some help. O cruel. O you gods.

Regan
One side will mock another. The other too.

Cornwall
If you see vengeance.

First Servant
                    Hold your hand, my lord.
I have served you ever since I was a child
But better service have I never done you
Than now to bid you hold.

Regan
                    How now, you dog.

First Servant
If you did wear a beard upon your chin
I'd shake it on this quarrel.

Cornwall
My villein.

First Servant
Nay then, come on, and take the chance of anger.

Regan
Give me thy sword. A peasant stand up thus.

First Servant
O, I am slain. My lord, you have one eye left
To see some mischief on him.

Cornwall
Lest it see more, prevent it. Out, vile jelly.
Where is thy lustre now?

Gloucester
All dark and comfortless. Where's my son Edmund?
Edmund, enkindle all the sparks of nature
To quit this horrid act.

Regan

                    Out, treacherous villain.
Thou call'st on him that hates thee. It was he
That made the overture of thy treasons to us
Who is too good to pity thee.

Gloucester

O my follies. Then Edgar was abused.
Kind gods, forgive me that and prosper him.

Regan

Go thrust him out at gates and let him smell
His way to Dover. How is it my lord? How look you?

Cornwall

I have received a hurt. Follow me lady.
Turn out that eyeless villain. Throw this slave
Upon the dunghill. Regan, I bleed apace.
Untimely comes this hurt. Give me your arm.

Second Servant

I'll never care what wickedness I do
If this man come to good.

Third Servant

                    If she live long
And in the end meet the old course of death
Women will all turn monsters.

Second Servant

Let's follow the old Earl and get the Bedlam
To lead him where he would. His roguish madness
Allows itself to any thing.

Third Servant

Go thou. I'll fetch some flax and whites of eggs
To apply to his bleeding face. Now heaven help him.

17

Edgar
Yet better thus and known to be condemned
Than still condemned and flattered. To be worst
The lowest and most dejected thing of fortune
Stands still in esperance, lives not in fear.
The lamentable change is from the best
The worst returns to laughter. Welcome then
Thou unsubstantial air that I embrace.
The wretch that thou hast blown unto the worst
Owes nothing to thy blasts. But who comes here?
My father poorly led? World, world, O world.

Gloucester
Away, get thee away, good friend, be gone.
Thy comforts can do me no good at all.
Thee they may hurt.

Servant
                        You cannot see your way.

Gloucester
I have no way and therefore want no eyes.
I stumbled when I saw. O dear son Edgar
The food of thy abused father's wrath
Might I but live to see thee in my touch
I'd say I had eyes again.

Servant
                        How now, who's there?

Edgar
O gods. Who is it can say 'I am at the worst'?
I am worse than e'er I was.

Servant
                        Tis poor mad Tom.

Edgar
And worse I may be yet. The worst is not
So long as we can say 'This is the worst.'

Servant
Fellow, where goest?

Gloucester
                              Is it a beggar man?

Servant
Madman and beggar too.

Gloucester
He has some reason, else he could not beg.
In the last night's storm I such a fellow saw
Which made me think a man a worm. My son
Came then into my mind, and yet my mind
Was then scarce friends with him. I have heard more since.
As flies to wanton boys, are we to the gods
They kill us for their sport.

Edgar
Bless thee, master.

Gloucester
Is that the naked fellow?

Servant
                              Ay, my lord.

Gloucester
Then prithee get thee gone. If for my sake
Thou wilt o'ertake us hence a mile or twain
In the way toward Dover, do it for ancient love
And bring some covering for this naked soul
Who I'll entreat to lead me.

Servant
                              Alack, sir, he is mad.

Gloucester
Tis the times plague when madmen lead the blind.
Do as I bid thee, or rather do thy pleasure.
Above the rest be gone.

Servant
I'll bring him the best apparel that I have,
Come on it what will.

Gloucester

Sirrah, naked fellow.

Edgar

Poor Tom's a-cold. I cannot daub it further.

Gloucester

Come hither, fellow.

Edgar

And yet I must. Bless thy sweet eyes, they bleed.

Gloucester

Knowest thou the way to Dover?

Edgar

Both stile and gate, horse-way and foot-path. Poor Tom
hath been scared out of his good wits. Bless thee, good
man's son, from the foul fiend.

Gloucester

Here, take this purse. That I am wretched
Makes thee the happier. Heavens, deal so still.
Let the superfluous and lust-dieted man
That slaves your ordinance, that will not see
Because he doth not feel, feel your power quickly.
So distribution should undo excess
And each man have enough. Dost thou know Dover?

Edgar

Ay, master.

Gloucester

There is a cliff whose high and bending head
Looks fearfully in the confined deep.
Bring me but to the very brim of it
And I'll repair the misery thou dost bear
With something rich about me. From that place
I shall no leading need.

Edgar

Give me thy arm.
Poor Tom shall lead thee.

18

Goneril
Welcome, my lord. I marvel our mild husband
Not met us on the way. Now where's your master?

Oswald
Madam within. But never man so changed.
I told him of the army that was landed.
He smiled at it. I told him you were coming.
His answer was 'the worse'. Of Gloucester's treachery
And of the loyal service of his son
When I informed him then he called me sot
And told me I had turned the wrong side out.

Goneril
Then shall you go no further.
It is the cowish terror of his spirit
That dares not undertake. Back, Edmund, to my brother.
Hasten his musters and conduct his powers
I must change arms at home and give the distaff
Into my husband's hands. This trusty servant
Shall pass between us. Ere long you are like to hear
If you dare venture in your own behalf
A mistress's command. Wear this, spare speech
Decline your head. This kiss, if it durst speak
Would stretch thy spirits up into the air.
Conceive and fare thee well.

Edmund
Yours in the ranks of death.

Goneril
                    My most dear Gloucester.
O the difference of man and man.
To thee a woman's services are due.
My fool usurps my body.

Oswald
                    Madam, here comes my lord.

Goneril
I have been worth the whistle.

Albany
                              O Goneril
You are not worth the dust which the rude wind
Blows in your face.

Goneril
No more. The text is foolish.

Albany
Wisdom and goodness to the vile seem vile.
Filths savour but themselves. What have you done?
Tigers, not daughters, what have you performed?
A father and a gracious aged man
Whose reverence even the head-lugged bear would lick
Most barbarous, most degenerate, have you madded.
If that the heavens do not their visible spirits
Send quickly down to tame these vile offences
It will come
Humanity must perforce prey on itself
Like monsters of the deep.

Goneril
                         Milk-livered man.
France spreads his banners in our noiseless land
Whiles thou, a moral fool, sit'st still and criest
'Alack, why does he so?'

Albany
                         See thyself, devil.
Proper deformity seems not in the fiend
So horrid as in woman.

Goneril
                    O vain fool.

Albany
Thou changed and self-covered thing for shame
Be-monster not thy feature. Were it my fitness
To let these hands obey my blood
They are apt enough to dislocate and tear

Thy flesh and bones. Howe'er thou art a fiend
A woman's shape doth shield thee.

Goneril
Marry your manhood, mew

Albany
What news?

Messenger
O my good lord, the Duke of Cornwall's dead.
Slain by his servant, going to put out
The other eye of Gloucester.

Albany
                              Gloucester's eyes?

Messenger
A servant that he bred, thrilled with remorse
Opposed against the act, bending his sword
To his great master. Who, thereat enraged
Flew on him and amongst them felled him dead.
But not without that harmful stroke, which since
Hath plucked him after.

Albany
                    This shows you are above
You justicers. But O, poor Gloucester
Lost he his other eye?

Messenger
                    Both, both my lord.
This letter, madam, craves a speedy answer.
Tis from your sister.

Goneril
                    One way I like this well.
But being widow and my Gloucester with her
The news is not so tart. I'll read and answer.

Albany
Where was his son when they did take his eyes?

Messenger
Come with my lady hither.

Albany
He is not here?

Messenger
No, my good lord, I met him back again.

Albany
Knows he the wickedness?

Messenger
Ay, my good lord. Twas he informed against him
And quit the house on purpose that their punishment
Might have the freer course.

Albany
                              Gloucester, I live
To thank thee for the love thou show'dst the King
And to revenge thine eyes. Come hither friend.
Tell me what more thou knowest.

19

Cordelia
Alack, tis he. Why he was met even now
As mad as the vexed sea. Singing aloud
Crowned with rank fumiter and furrow-weeds
With burdocks, hemlock, nettles, cuckoo-flowers
Darnel, and all the idle weeds that grow
In our sustaining corn. The centuries send forth.
Search every acre in the high-grown field
And bring him to our eye. What can man's wisdom
In the restoring his bereaved sense?
He that can help him take all my outward worth.

Gentleman
There is means, madam.
Our foster-nurse of nature is repose
The which he lacks. That to provoke in him

Are many simples operative, whose power
Will close the eye of anguish.

Cordelia
                        All blest secrets
All you unpublished virtues of the earth
Spring with my tears. Be aidant and remediate
In the good man's distress. Seek, seek for him
Lest his ungoverned rage dissolve his life
That wants the means to lead it.

Messenger
                            News, madam.
The British powers are marching hitherward.

Cordelia
Tis known before. Our preparation stands
In expectation of them. O dear father
It is thy business that I go about.
Therefore great France
My mourning and importunate tears hath pitied.
No blown ambition doth our arms incite
But love, dear love, and our aged father's right.
Soon may I hear and see him.

20

Regan
But are my brother's powers set forth?

Oswald
Ay, madam.

Regan
Himself in person there?

Oswald
Madam, with much ado.
Your sister is the better soldier.

Regan
Lord Edmund spake not with your lord at home?

Oswald
No, madam.

Regan
What might import my sister's letter to him?

Oswald
I know not, lady.

Regan
Faith, he is posted hence on serious matter.
It was great ignorance, Gloucester's eyes being out
To let him live. Where he arrives he moves
All hearts against us. Edmund, I think, is gone
In pity of his misery to dispatch
His nighted life. Moreover to descry
The strength of the enemy.

Oswald
I must needs after him, madam, with my letter.

Regan
Our troops set forth tomorrow. Stay with us.
The ways are dangerous.

Oswald
                I may not, madam.
My lady charged my duty in this business.

Regan
Why should she write to Edmund? Might not you
Transport her purposes by word? Belike
Something I know not what. I'll love thee much
Let me unseal the letter.

Oswald
                Madam, I had rather –

Regan
I know your lady does not love her husband.
I am sure of that. And at her late being here
She gave strange oeillades and most speaking looks
To noble Edmund. I know you are of her bosom.

Oswald
I madam?

Regan
I speak in understanding. You are, I know it.
Therefore I do advise you take this note.
My lord is dead. Edmund and I have talked
And more convenient is he for my hand
Than for your lady's. You may gather more.
If you do find him, pray you, give him this.
And when your mistress hears thus much from you
I pray desire her call her wisdom to her.
So farewell.
If you do chance to hear of that blind traitor
Preferment falls on him that cuts him off.

Oswald
Would I could meet him madam. I would show
What lady I do follow.

Regan
Fare thee well.

21

Gloucester
When shall we come to the top of that same hill?

Edgar
You do climb up it now. Look how we labour.

Gloucester
Methinks the ground is even.

Edgar
                              Horrible steep.
Hark, do you hear the sea?

Gloucester
                              No truly.

Edgar
Why then your other senses grow imperfect
By your eyes anguish.

Gloucester
So may it be indeed.
Methinks thy voice is altered and thou speakst
In better phrase and matter than thou didst.

Edgar
You're much deceived. In nothing am I changed
But in my garments.

Gloucester
Methinks you're better spoken.

Edgar
Come on sir, here's the place. Stand still. How fearful
And dizzy tis to cast one's eyes so low.
The crows and choughs that wing the midway air
Show scarce so gross as beetles. Half way down
Hangs one that gathers samphire, dreadful trade.
Methinks he seems no bigger than his head.
The fishermen that walk upon the beach
Appear like mice and yond tall anchoring bark
Diminished to her cock, her cock a buoy
Almost too small for sight. The murmuring surge
That on the unnumbered idle pebbles chafes
Cannot be heard so high. I'll look no more
Lest my brain turn, and the deficient sight
Topple down headlong.

Gloucester
Set me where you stand.

Edgar
Give me your hand. You are now within a foot
Of the extreme verge. For all beneath the moon
Would I not leap upright.

Gloucester
Let go my hand.
Here friend's another purse. In it a jewel

Well worth a poor man's taking. Go thou farther off.
Bid me farewell, and let me hear thee going.

Edgar
Now fare you well, good sir.

Gloucester
With all my heart.

Edgar
Why I do trifle thus with his despair
Is done to cure it.

Gloucester
O you mighty gods
This world I do renounce, and in your sights
Shake patiently my great affliction off.
If I could bear it longer and not fall
To quarrel with your great opposeless wills
My snuff and loathed part of nature should
Burn itself out. If Edgar live, O bless him.
Now, fellow, fare thee well.

Edgar
Gone, sir, farewell.
Had he been where he thought
By this had thought been past. Alive or dead?
Ho, you sir. Hear you, sir, speak.
Thus might he pass indeed. Yet he revives.
What are you, sir?

Gloucester
Away and let me die.

Edgar
Hadst thou been aught but gossamer, feathers, air
So many fathom down precipitating
Thou'dst shivered like an egg. But thou dost breathe
Hast heavy substance, bleedst not, speakst, art sound.
Ten masts at length make not the altitude
Which thou hast perpendicularly fell.
Thy life's a miracle. Speak yet again.

Gloucester
But have I fallen, or no?

Edgar
From the dread summit of this chalky bourn.
Look up a-height. The shrill-gorged lark so far
Cannot be seen or heard. Do but look up.

Gloucester
Alack, I have no eyes.
Is wretchedness deprived that benefit
To end itself by death? Twas yet some comfort
When misery could beguile the tyrant's rage
And frustrate his proud will.

Edgar
Give me your arm.
Up. So. How is it? Feel you your legs? You stand.

Gloucester
Too well, too well.

Edgar
This is above all strangeness.
Upon the crown of the cliff, what thing was that
Which parted from you?

Gloucester
A poor unfortunate beggar.

Edgar
As I stood here below methought his eyes
Were two full moons. He had a thousand noses
Horns whelked and waved like the enridged sea.
It was some fiend. Therefore, thou happy father
Think that the clearest gods, who make them honours
Of men's impossibilities, have preserved thee.

Gloucester
I do remember now. Henceforth I'll bear
Affliction till it do cry out itself
'Enough, enough' and die.

Edgar
Bear free and patient thoughts. But who comes here?

Lear
No, they cannot touch me for coining. I am the King himself.

Edgar
O thou side-piercing sight.

Lear
Nature's above art in that respect. There's your press-money. That fellow handles his bow like a crow-keeper. Draw me a clothier's yard. Look, look, a mouse. Peace, peace. This piece of toasted cheese will do it. There's my gauntlet. I'll prove it on a giant. Bring up the brown bills. O, well flown, bird. In the cloud, in the cloud. Give the word.

Edgar
Sweet marjoram.

Lear
Pass.

Gloucester
I know that voice.

Lear
Ha. Goneril, with a white beard. They flattered me like a dog, and told me I had white hairs in my beard ere the black ones were there. When the rain came to wet me once, and the wind to make me chatter, when the thunder would not peace at my bidding, there I found 'em, there I smelt 'em out. Go to, they are not men of their words. They told me I was everything. Tis a lie, I am not ague-proof.

Gloucester
The trick of that voice I do well remember.
Is it not the King?

Lear

                    Ay, every inch a King.
When I do stare, see how the subject quakes.
I pardon that man's life. What was thy cause?
Adultery? Thou shalt not die for adultery.
No, the wren goes to it and the small gilded fly
Does lecher in my sight.
Let copulation thrive, for Gloucester's bastard son
Was kinder to his father than my daughters
Got tween the lawful sheets.
To it luxury, pell·mell, for I lack soldiers.
Behold yond simpering dame
Whose face between her forks presages snow
That minces virtue and does shake the head
To hear of pleasure's name.
The fitchew nor the soiled horse goes to it
With a more riotous appetite.
Down from the waist they are Centaurs
Though women all above.
But to the girdle do the gods inherit.
Beneath is all the fiends.
There's hell, there's darkness, there's the sulphurous pit,
burning, scalding, stench, consumption. Give me an
ounce of civet, good apothecary, to sweeten my
imagination. There's money for thee.

Gloucester
O, let me kiss that hand.

Lear
Let me wipe it first. It smells of mortality.

Gloucester
O ruined piece of nature. This great world
Shall so wear out to nought. Do you know me?

Lear
I remember thy eyes well enough. Dost thou squiny at
me? No, do thy worst, blind Cupid, I'll not love. Read thou
this challenge. Mark but the penning of it.

Gloucester
Were all the letters suns, I could not see one.

Edgar
I would not take this from report. It is
And my heart breaks at it.

Lear
Read.

Gloucester
What, with the case of eyes?

Lear
Oho, are you there with me? No eyes in your head, nor no
money in your purse? Your eyes are in a heavy case,
your purse in a light. Yet you see how this world goes.

Gloucester
I see it feelingly.

Lear
What, art mad? A man may see how this world goes with
no eyes. Look with thine ears. See how yon justice rails
upon yon simple thief. Hark in thy ear. Change places and
handy-dandy, which is the justice, which is the thief?
Thou hast seen a farmer's dog bark at a beggar?

Gloucester
Ay, sir.

Lear
And the creature run from the cur? There thou mightst
behold the great image of authority. A dog's obeyed in
office.
Thou rascal beadle, hold thy bloody hand.
Why dost thou lash that whore? Strip thine own back.
Thou hotly lustst to use her in that kind
For which thou whippst her.
Through tattered clothes small vices do appear.
Robes and furred gowns hide all. Plate sin with gold
And the strong lance of justice hurtless breaks.
Arm it in rags a pigmy's straw does pierce it.

Get thee glass eyes
And like a scurvy politician seem
To see the things thou dost not. Now, now, now, now.
Pull off my boots. Harder, harder, so.

Edgar
O matter and impertinency mixed.
Reason in madness.

Lear
If thou wilt weep my fortunes take my eyes.
I know thee well enough. Thy name is Gloucester.
Thou must be patient. We came crying hither.
Thou knowest the first time that we smell the air
We wawl and cry. I will preach to thee, mark.

Gloucester
Alack, alack the day.

Lear
When we are born we cry that we are come
To this great stage of fools. This is a good block.
It were a delicate stratagem to shoe
A troop of horse with felt. I'll put it in proof
And when I have stolen upon these sons-in-law
Then kill, kill, kill, kill, kill, kill.

Gentleman
O here he is. Lay hand upon him. Sir
Your most dear –

Lear
No rescue? What, a prisoner? I am even
The natural fool of fortune. Use me well.
You shall have ransom. Let me have surgeons
I am cut to the brains.

Gentleman
You shall have anything.

Lear
No seconds? All myself?
Why this would make a man a man of salt

To use his eyes for garden water-pots
Ay and laying autumn's dust.

Gentleman
Good sir.

Lear
I will die bravely like a smug bridegroom.
What, I will be jovial. Come, come
I am a King, my masters, know you that?

Gentleman
You are a royal one, and we obey you.

Lear
Then there's life in it. Nay, an you get it, you shall get it
with running.

Edgar
Hail, gentle sir.
Do you hear aught of a battle toward?

Gentleman
Every one hears that.

Edgar
How near's the other army?

Gentleman
Near and on speedy foot.

Edgar
I thank you, sir.

Gloucester
You ever-gentle gods take my breath from me.
Let not my worser spirit tempt me again
To die before you please.

Edgar
                              Well pray you, father.

Gloucester
Now, good sir, what are you?

Edgar
A most poor man, made lame to fortune's blows
Who, by the art of known and feeling sorrows
Am pregnant to good pity. Give me your hand.
I'll lead you to some biding.

Gloucester
                                        Hearty thanks.

Oswald
A proclaimed prize. Most happy.
That eyeless head of thine was first framed flesh
To raise my fortunes. Thou most unhappy traitor
Briefly thyself remember. The sword is out
That must destroy thee.

Gloucester
                                Now let thy friendly hand
Put strength enough to it.

Oswald
                                Wherefore, bold peasant
Darest thou support a published traitor? Hence
Lest that the infection of his fortune take
Like hold on thee. Let go his arm.

Edgar
I'll not let go, sir, without further occasion.

Oswald
Let go, slave, or thou diest.

Edgar
Good gentleman, go your gait, and let poor folk pass.
Nay, come not near the old man, or I shall try whether
your costard or my ballow be the harder. I'll be plain with
you.

Oswald
Out, dunghill.

Edgar
I'll pick your teeth, sir. Come, no matter for your foins.

Oswald
Slave, thou hast slain me. Villain, take my purse.
If ever thou wilt thrive, bury my body
And give the letters which thou findst about me
To Edmund, Earl of Gloucester. Seek him out
Upon the British party. O untimely death.

Edgar
I know thee well. A serviceable villain
As duteous to the vices of thy mistress
As badness would desire.

Gloucester
               Is he dead?

Edgar
Sit you down, father, rest you.
Let's see these pockets. The letters that he speaks of
may be my friends. He's dead. I am only sorry he had no
other deathsman. Let us see.
'Let our reciprocal vows be remembered. You have many
opportunities to cut him off. There is nothing done, if he
return the conqueror. Then am I the prisoner and his bed
my gaol. From the loathed warmth whereof deliver me,
and supply the place for your labour. Your – wife, so I
would say – affectionate servant, Goneril.'
O undistinguished space of woman's wit.
A plot upon her virtuous husband's life
And the exchange my brother.

Gloucester
The King is mad. Better I were distraught.
So should my thoughts be severed from my griefs
And woes by wrong imaginations lose
The knowledge of themselves.

Edgar
                       Give me your hand.
Far off methinks I hear the beaten drum
Come, father, I'll bestow you with a friend.

22

Cordelia
O thou good Kent
How shall I live and work to match thy goodness?
My life will be too short and every measure fail me.

Kent
To be acknowledged, madam, is o'erpaid.
All my reports go with the modest truth.
Nor more nor clipped, but so.

Cordelia
                        Be better suited.
These weeds are memories of those worser hours.
I prithee, put them off.

Kent
                        Pardon me, dear madam.
Yet to be known shortens my made intent.
My boon I make it that you know me not
Till time and I think meet.

Cordelia
Then be it so my good lord.
How does the King?

Gentleman
                    Madam, sleeps still.

Cordelia
                                    O you kind gods
Cure this great breach in his abused nature.

Gentleman
So please your majesty
That we may wake the King. He hath slept long.

Cordelia
Be governed by your knowledge and proceed
In the sway of your own will. Is he arrayed?

Kent
Ay madam. In the heaviness of his sleep
We put fresh garments on him.

Gentleman
Good madam, be by when we do awake him.
I doubt not of his temperance.

Cordelia
                                    Very well.

Gentleman
Please you draw near.

Cordelia
O my dear father, restoration hang
Thy medicine on my lips and let this kiss
Repair those violent harms that my two sisters
Have in thy reverence made.

Kent
                          Kind and dear princess.

Cordelia
Had you not been their father, these white flakes
Had challenged pity of them. Was this a face
To be exposed against the warring winds?
To stand against the deep dread-bolted thunder
In the most terrible and nimble stroke
Of quick, cross lightning? Mine enemy's dog
Though he had bit me, should have stood that night
Against my fire. Alack, alack
Tis wonder that thy life and wits at once
Had not concluded all. He wakes. Speak to him.

Gentleman
Madam, do you. Tis fittest.

Cordelia
How does my royal lord? How fares your majesty?

Lear
You do me wrong to take me out of the grave.
Thou art a soul in bliss, but I am bound

Upon a wheel of fire, that mine own tears
Do scald like molten lead.

Cordelia

Sir, do you know me?

Lear
You're a spirit I know. When did you die?

Cordelia
Still, still, far wide.

Gentleman
He's scarce awake. Let him alone awhile.

Lear
Where have I been? Where am I? Fair daylight?
I am mightily abused. I should even die with pity
To see another thus. I know not what to say.
I will not swear these are my hands. Let's see.
I feel this pin prick. Would I were assured
Of my condition.

Cordelia

O look upon me, sir
And hold your hands in benediction o'er me.
No, sir, you must not kneel.

Lear
Pray do not mock me.
I am a very foolish, fond old man
Fourscore and upward
Not an hour more nor less and to deal plainly
I fear I am not in my perfect mind.
Methinks I should know you and know this man.
Yet I am doubtful, for I am mainly ignorant
What place this is and all the skill I have
Remembers not these garments, nor I know not
Where I did lodge last night. Do not laugh at me
For as I am a man, I think this lady
To be my child Cordelia.

Cordelia

And so I am, I am.

Lear

Be your tears wet? Yes, faith, I pray weep not.
If you have poison for me I will drink it.
I know you do not love me, for your sisters
Have as I do remember done me wrong.
You have some cause, they have not.

Cordelia

No cause, no cause.

Lear

Am I in France?

Kent

In your own kingdom, sir.

Lear

Do not abuse me.

Gentleman

Be comforted, good madam. The great rage
You see is cured in him. And yet it is danger
To make him even o'er the time he has lost.
Desire him to go in. Trouble him no more
Till further settling.

Cordelia

Will it please your Highness walk?

Lear

You must bear with me.
Pray now, forget and forgive. I am old and foolish.

23

Edmund

Know of the Duke if his last purpose hold
Or whether since he is advised by aught
To change the course. He's full of alteration
And self-reproving. Bring his constant pleasure.

Regan
Our sister's man is certainly miscarried.

Edmund
Tis to be feared, madam.

Regan
                              Now sweet lord
You know the goodness I intend upon you.
Tell me but truly, but then speak the truth
Do you not love my sister?

Edmund
                              In honoured love.

Regan
But have you never found my brother's way
To the forfended place?

Edmund
                    That thought abuses you.

Regan
I am fearful that you have been conjunct
And bosomed with her.

Edmund
No, by mine honour, madam.

Regan
I never shall endure her. Dear my lord
Be not familiar with her.

Edmund
                         Fear me not.
She and the Duke her husband.

Goneril
I had rather lose the battle than that sister
Should loosen him and me.

Albany
Our very loving sister well be-met.
Sir, this I hear. The King is come to his daughter
With others whom the rigor of our state

Forced to cry out. Where I could not be honest
I never yet was valiant. For this business
It toucheth us as France invades our land.
Yet bold's the King with others whom I fear
Most just and heavy causes make oppose.

Edmund
Sir, you speak nobly.

Regan
               Why is this reasoned?

Goneril
Combine together gainst the enemy.
For these domestic poor particular broils
Are not to question here.

Albany
               Let's then determine
With the ensign of war on our proceedings.

Edmund
I shall attend you presently at your tent.

Regan
Sister, you'll go with us?

Goneril
No.

Regan
Tis most convenient. Pray you, go with us.

Goneril
O, ho, I know the riddle. I will go.

Edgar
If e'er your grace had speech with man so poor
Hear me one word.

Albany
             I'll overtake you. Speak.

Edgar
Before you fight the battle ope this letter.
If you have victory let the trumpet sound

For him that brought it. Wretched though I seem
I can produce a champion that will prove
What is avouched there. Fortune love you.

Albany
Stay till I have read the letter.

Edgar
I was forbid it.
When time shall serve let but the herald cry
And I'll appear again.

Albany
Why fare thee well. I will o'erlook thy paper.

Edmund
The enemy's in view. Draw up your powers.
Here is the guess of their true strength and forces
By diligent discovery. But your haste
Is now urged on you.

Albany
We will greet the time.

Edmund
To both these sisters have I sworn my love.
Each jealous of the other, as the stung
Are of the adder. Which of them shall I take?
Both? one? or neither? Neither can be enjoyed
If both remain alive. To take the widow
Exasperates, makes mad her sister Goneril
And hardly shall I carry out my side
Her husband being alive. Now then we'll use
His countenance for the battle, which being done
Let her who would be rid of him devise
His speedy taking off. As for his mercy
Which he intends to Lear and to Cordelia
The battle done, and they within our power
Shall never see his pardon. For my state
Stands on me to defend, not to debate.

24

Edgar
Here, father, take the shadow of this tree
For your good host. Pray that the right may thrive.
If ever I return to you again
I'll bring you comfort.

Gloucester
                        Grace go with you, sir.

Edgar
Away, old man, give me thy hand, away.
King Lear hath lost. He and his daughter taken.
Give me thy hand, come on.

Gloucester
No farther sir. A man may rot even here.

Edgar
What, in ill thoughts again? Men must endure
Their going hence even as their coming hither.
Ripeness is all. Come on.

Gloucester
                        And that's true too.

25

Edmund
Some officers take them away. Good guard
Until their greater pleasures first be known
That are to censure them.

Cordelia
                        We are not the first
Who with best meaning have incurred the worst.
For thee, oppressed King, am I cast down.
Myself could else out-frown false fortune's frown.
Shall we not see these daughters and these sisters?

Lear
No, no, no, no. Come, let's away to prison.
We two alone will sing like birds in the cage.
When thou dost ask me blessing, I'll kneel down
And ask of thee forgiveness. So we'll live
And pray and sing and tell old tales and laugh
At gilded butterflies and hear poor rogues
Talk of court news, and we'll talk with them too
Who loses and who wins, who's in, who's out
And take upon us the mystery of things
As if we were God's spies. And we'll wear out
In a walled prison pacts and sects of great ones
That ebb and flow by the moon.

Edmund
                              Take them away.

Lear
Upon such sacrifices, my Cordelia
The gods themselves throw incense. Have I caught thee?
He that parts us shall bring a brand from heaven
And fire us hence like foxes. Wipe thine eyes
The good years shall devour them, flesh and fell
Ere they shall make us weep. We'll see 'em starve first.
Come.

Edmund
          Come hither, Captain, hark.
Take thou this note. Go follow them to prison.
One step I have advanced thee. If thou dost
As this instructs thee, thou dost make thy way
To noble fortunes. Know thou this, that men
Are as the time is. To be tender-minded
Does not become a sword. Either say thou'lt do it
Or thrive by other means.

Captain
                    I'll do it, my lord.

Edmund
About it, and write happy when thou hast done.

Captain
I cannot draw a cart nor eat dried oats.
If it be man's work, I'll do it.

Albany
Sir, you have shown today your valiant strain
And fortune led you well. You have the captives
That were the opposites of this day's strife.
We do require them of you, so to use them
As we shall find their merits and our safety
May equally determine.

Edmund
                              Sir, I thought it fit
To send the old and miserable King
To some retention and appointed guard.
With him I sent the Queen. And they are ready
Tomorrow or at further space to appear
Where you shall hold your session. At this time
We sweat and bleed. The friend hath lost his friend
And the best quarrels in the heat are cursed
By those that feel their sharpness.
The question of Cordelia and her father
Requires a fitter place.

Albany
                              Sir, by your patience
I hold you but a subject of this war
Not as a brother.

Regan
                      That's as we list to grace him.
Methinks our pleasure might have been demanded
Ere you had spoke so far. He led our powers
Bore the commission of my place and person.
The which immediacy may well stand up
And call itself your brother.

Goneril
                              Not so hot.
In his own grace he doth exalt himself
More than in your advancement.

Regan

In my right
By me invested, he compeers the best.

Goneril

That were the most if he should husband you.

Regan

Jesters do oft prove prophets.

Goneril

Holla, holla
That eye that told you so looked but asquint.

Regan

Lady, I am not well else I should answer
From a full-flowing stomach. General
Take thou my soldiers, prisoners, patrimony.
Witness the world that I create thee here
My lord and master.

Goneril

Mean you to enjoy him?

Albany

The let-alone lies not in your good will.

Edmund

Nor in thine, lord.

Albany

Half-blooded fellow, yes.

Regan

Let the drum strike and prove my title thine.

Albany

Stay yet. Hear reason. Edmund, I arrest thee
On capital treason and in thine attaint
This gilded serpent. For your claim, fair sister
I bar it in the interest of my wife.
Tis she is sub-contracted to this lord
And I her husband contradict your banns.
If you will marry make your loves to me.
My lady is bespoke.

Goneril
> An interlude.

Albany
Thou art armed, Gloucester. Let the trumpet sound.
If none appear to prove upon thy head
Thy heinous, manifest, and many treasons
There is my pledge, I'll prove it on thy heart
Ere I taste bread, thou art in nothing less
Than I have here proclaimed thee.

Regan
Sick, oh sick.

Goneril
If not, I'll ne'er trust poison.

Edmund
There's my exchange. What in the world he is
That names me traitor, villain-like he lies.
Call by the trumpet.

Albany
> A herald, ho.
Trust to thy single virtue, for thy soldiers
All levied in my name, have in my name
Took their discharge.

Regan
> My sickness grows upon me.

Albany
Come hither, herald. Let the trumpet sound
And read out this.

Herald
'If any man of quality or degree within the lists of the
army will maintain upon Edmund, supposed Earl of
Gloucester, that he is a manifold traitor, let him appear
by the third sound of the trumpet. He is bold in his
defence.'

Edmund
Sound.

Herald
Again. Again.

Albany
Ask him his purposes, why he appears
Upon this call of the trumpet.

Herald
                              What are you?
Your name, your quality, and why you answer
This present summons?

Edgar
                              Know my name is lost.
Yet am I noble as the adversary
I come to cope.

Albany
                    Which is that adversary?

Edgar
What's he that speaks for Edmund Earl of Gloucester?

Edmund
Himself. What say'st thou to him?

Edgar
                                        Draw thy sword.
That if my speech offend a noble heart
Thy arm may do thee justice. Here is mine.
Behold it is the privilege of my tongue
My oath and my profession. I protest
Maugre thy strength, youth, place and eminence
Despite thy victor sword and fire new fortune
Thy valour and thy heart, thou art a traitor
False to thy gods, thy brother and thy father
Conspirant gainst this high illustrious prince
And from the extremest upward of thy head
To the descent and dust beneath thy feet
A most toad spotted traitor. Say thou no
This sword, this arm and my best spirits are bent
To prove upon thy heart whereto I speak
Thou liest.

Edmund
                    In wisdom I should ask thy name.
But since thy outside looks so fair and warlike
And that thy tongue some say of breeding breathes
My right of knighthood I disdain and spurn.
Here do I toss these treasons to thy head
With the hell-hated lie o'erwhelm thy heart
Which for they yet glance by and scarcely bruise
This sword of mine shall give them instant way
Where they shall rest for ever. Trumpets, speak.

Albany
Save him, save him.

Goneril
                    This is practice, Gloucester.
By the law of arms thou wast not bound to answer
An unknown opposite. Thou art not vanquished
But cozened and beguiled.

Albany
                              Shut your mouth, dame
Or with this paper shall I stop it.
Thou worse than anything, read thine own evil.
Nay, no tearing, lady. I perceive you know it.

Goneril
Say if I do, the laws are mine not thine.
Who shall arraign me for it?

Albany
                              Most monstrous.
Know'st thou this paper?

Goneril
                    Ask me not what I know.

Edmund
What you have charged me with, that have I done
And more, much more. The time will bring it out.
Tis past, and so am I. But what art thou
That hast this fortune on me? If thou beest noble
I do forgive thee.

Edgar

Let's exchange charity.
I am no less in blood than thou art, Edmund.
If more, the more thou hast wronged me.
My name is Edgar, and thy father's son.

Edmund
The wheel is come full circle. I am here.

Albany
Methought thy very gait did prophesy
A royal nobleness. I must embrace thee.
Let sorrow split my heart if I did ever
Hate thee or thy father.

Edgar

Worthy prince, I know it.

Albany
Where have you hid yourself?
How have you known the miseries of your father?

Edgar
By nursing them, my lord. List a brief tale
And when tis told, O that my heart would burst.
The bloody proclamation taught me to shift
Into a madman's rags. And in this habit
Met I my father with his bleeding rings.
Their precious stones new lost, became his guide.
Led him, begged for him, saved him from despair.
Never, O father, revealed myself unto him
Until some half-hour past, when I was armed.
Not sure, though hoping, of this good success
I asked his blessing, and from first to last
Told him my pilgrimage. But his flawed heart
Alack too weak the conflict to support
Twixt two extremes of passion, joy and grief
Burst smilingly.

Edmund

This speech of yours hath moved me
And shall perchance do good. But speak you on.

Edgar
Whilst I was big in clamour came there in a man
Who having seen me in my worst estate
Shunned my abhorred society. But then finding
Who it was that so endured, with his strong arms
He fastened on my neck and told
The most piteous tale of Lear and him
That ever ear received.

Albany
                              But who was this?

Edgar
Kent, sir, the banished Kent, who in disguise
Followed his enemy King and did him service
Improper for a slave.

Gentleman
                              Help, help.

Albany
What means this bloody knife?

Gentleman
                                        It's hot, it smokes.
It came even from the heart of –

Albany
                                   Who man? Speak.

Gentleman
Your lady, sir, your lady. And her sister
By her is poisoned. She hath confessed it.

Edmund
I was contracted to them both. All three
Now marry in an instant.

Albany
Produce their bodies be they alive or dead.
This judgment of the heavens that makes us tremble
Touches us not with pity.

Edgar
                              Here comes Kent.

Kent
I am come
To bid my King and master aye good night.
Is he not here?

Albany
                    Great thing of us forgot.
Speak, Edmund. Where's the King and where's Cordelia?
See'st thou this object, Kent?

Kent
                                Alack, why thus?

Edmund
Yet Edmund was beloved.
The one the other poisoned for my sake
And after slew herself.

Albany
                        Even so. Cover their faces.

Edmund
I pant for life. Some good I mean to do
Despite of mine own nature. Quickly send
Be brief in't, to the castle, for my writ
Is on the life of Lear and on Cordelia.
Nay, send in time.

Albany
                    Run, run, O run.

Edgar
To who, my lord? Who hath the office? Send
Thy token of reprieve.

Edmund
                    Take my sword.
Give it the captain.

Albany
                        Haste thee, for thy life.

Edmund
He hath commission from thy wife and me
To hang Cordelia in the prison and

To lay the blame upon her own despair
That she fordid herself.

Albany
The gods defend her. Bear him hence awhile.

Lear
Howl, howl, howl, howl. O, you are men of stones.
Had I your tongues and eyes, I'd use them so
That heaven's vault should crack. She's gone for ever.
I know when one is dead and when one lives.
She's dead as earth. Lend me a looking-glass.
If that her breath will mist or stain the stone
Why then she lives.

Kent
Is this the promised end?

Edgar
Or image of that horror?

Albany
Fall and cease.

Lear
This feather stirs. She lives. If it be so
It is a chance which does redeem all sorrows
That ever I have felt.

Kent
O my good master.

Lear
Prithee, away.

Edgar
Tis noble Kent, your friend.

Lear
A plague upon you murderous traitors all.
I might have saved her. Now she's gone for ever.
Cordelia, Cordelia, stay a little. Ha?
What is't thou say'st? Her voice was ever soft
Gentle and low, an excellent thing in woman.
I killed the slave that was a-hanging thee.

Captain
Tis true, my lords, he did.

Lear
                          Did I not, fellow?
I have seen the day with my good biting falchion
I would have made them skip. I am old now
And these same crosses spoil me. Who are you?
Mine eyes are not of the best, I'll tell you straight.

Kent
If Fortune brag of two she loved or hated
One of them we behold.

Lear
                          Are you not Kent?

Kent
The same. Your servant Kent.
Where is your servant Caius?

Lear
He's a good fellow, I can tell you that.
He'll strike, and quickly too. He's dead and rotten.

Kent
No, my good lord, I am the very man –

Lear
I'll see that straight.

Kent
That from your first of difference and decay
Have followed your sad steps.

Lear
                          You're welcome hither.

Kent
Nor no man else. All's cheerless, dark and deadly.
Your eldest daughters have fordone themselves
And desperately are dead.

Lear
                          So think I too.

Albany
He knows not what he sees and vain it is
That we present us to him.

Edgar

                        Very bootless.

Captain
Edmund is dead, my lord.

Albany

                        That's but a trifle here.
You lords and noble friends know our intent.
What comfort to this great decay may come
Shall be applied. For us we will resign
During the life of this old majesty
To him our absolute power. You to your rights
With boot and such addition as your honours
Have more than merited. All friends shall taste
The wages of their virtue, and all foes
The cup of their deservings. O see, see.

Lear
And my poor fool is hanged. No, no, no life.
Why should a dog, a horse, a rat, have life
And thou no breath at all? Thou'lt come no more
Never, never, never, never, never.
Pray you undo this button. Thank you, sir.
Do you see this? Look on her, look her lips.
Look there, look there.

Edgar
My lord, my lord.

Kent
Break heart, I prithee, break.

Edgar
Look up, my lord.

Kent
Vex not his ghost. O let him pass. He hates him
That would upon the rack of this tough world
Stretch him out longer.

Edgar

He is gone indeed.

Kent

The wonder is he hath endured so long.
He but usurped his life.

Albany

Bear them from hence. Our present business
Is general woe. Friends of my soul, you twain
Rule in this realm and the gored state sustain.

Kent

I have a journey, sir, shortly to go
My master calls and I must not say no.

Edgar

The weight of this sad time we must obey
Speak what we feel, not what we ought to say.
The oldest hath borne most. We that are young
Shall never see so much, nor live so long.